SAMUEL BECKETT

A NEW APPROACH

*By the same author*

THE PSYCHOLOGY OF THE POET SHELLEY
(with Edward Carpenter and under the
pseudonym of George Barnefield)

THE SUPERNORMAL

# Samuel Beckett
# A New Approach

## A Study of the Novels and Plays

*by*

*G. C. Barnard*

*Ha! here's three on's are sophisticated; thou art
the thing itself; unaccommodated man is no more
but such a poor, bare, forked animal as thou art.
Off, off, you lendings!*

(*King Lear, III, iv*)

LONDON
J. M. DENT & SONS LTD

First published March 1970
Reprinted May 1970

Made in Great Britain
at the
Bowering Press · Plymouth
for
J. M. DENT & SONS LTD
Aldine House · Bedford Street · London

ISBN 0 460 03918 0

*To*

BETTY – MICHAEL – MEG

*whose encouragement and help have made this book*

*possible*

# Contents

# *Acknowledgements*

My thanks for permissions to quote from various authors are due to the following publishers and agents:

To Calder & Boyars Ltd., Faber & Faber, The Grove Press Inc., and Rosica Colin Ltd for the numerous quotations from Samuel Beckett's novels and plays; to Faber & Faber Ltd and The Sterling Lord Agency for a sentence from Jacobsen & Mueller's *The Testament of Beckett*; to The Hogarth Press, Sigmund Freud's Copyrights Ltd., The Institute of Psycho-Analysis and W. W. Norton Inc., in respect of the quotation from Vol. XXII of the Standard Edition of the *Complete Psychological Works of S. Freud*; to Constable & Co. and The Society of Authors, as Agent for the Bernard Shaw Estate, for one from the Preface to *Immaturity*; to George Allen & Unwin Ltd for a sentence from Edward Carpenter's *Toward Democracy*; To Tavistock Publications Ltd for one from Dr D. Cooper's *Psychiatry and Antipsychiatry*; to the Editor of the Journal of the Society for Psychical Research for a quotation from Prof. C. D. Broad's *Myers Memorial Lecture* (1958); to André Deutsch for one from Peggy Guggenheim's *Confessions of an Art Addict*; and to Chatto & Windus Ltd and Barnes & Noble Inc. for one from John Fletcher's *The Novels of Samuel Beckett*.

Finally I would like to thank Mr John Calder for some helpful suggestions and Mr B. P. Jones, of the Sheffield University Library, for his assistance in finding the exact wording of the quotation from Freud.

# Preface

THE WORKS OF SAMUEL BECKETT, by the strangeness of their content and their stylistic novelty, undoubtedly present many difficulties to the unprepared reader, but they are very relevant to our twentieth-century situation and they repay careful and repeated reading. Beckett's tramps and outcasts, in all their fantastic settings, are concerned with the old problems of time and eternity, of human suffering, and of the purpose and nature of the real self within. Contemporary man accepts neither the old religious answers nor the pseudo-scientific answers of the materialist; he is searching for a new, specifically human answer. Beckett does not provide one, but he does present the questions in a new way and thereby enlarges our awareness and helps us towards a greater insight.

The work of any deeply imaginative writer, and particularly one who uses symbols and deliberate ambiguities as Beckett does, permits of various conflicting interpretations and has different levels of meaning which may all be equally justified. Several such studies have been made, notably the works by Professor Hugh Kenner, R. N. Coe, Jacobsen and Mueller, and John Fletcher which are listed in the bibliography. These have shed much light on the metaphysical aspects of Beckett's works and on their literary forms and qualities, but in my view they fail to deal adequately with the psychological and purely human aspects, and notably they entirely ignore the part played by schizophrenia in the novels. Without an appreciation of this one cannot fully understand the plays or the novels. A host of discrepancies in the narratives and of apparently irrelevant details or remarks, which these commentators have either ignored or treated as wanton enigmas inserted at the caprice of the author, become meaningful when the schizophrenic situation is understood.

The favourite question put by the reader or playgoer confronted by a work of Beckett's is 'what does it mean?' To this there is no single answer. The novel or the play is a poetic presentation of something the author has perceived or imagined; it is full of meanings, but it does not convey a neat religious, philosophical or social lesson which can be stated in a formula. Its meaning is what the reader finds in it for himself.

I have tried to expound the meanings which I have found in these works in the hope that the general reader will be led on to explore them for himself and discover that they have significance for him.

As this book is meant to be a popular introduction, not an academic treatise, I have confined myself to the works which are available in English and have not considered the minor differences between the French and English texts of certain works.

While this book was in the printer's hands it was announced that Samuel Beckett had been awarded the Nobel Prize for literature for 1969. Thus he joins that elite international band of authors which already includes two fellow Irishmen, Bernard Shaw and W. B. Yeats.

# PART 1

## *The Novels*

# Introduction

SAMUEL BECKETT was born in Dublin in 1906 and so his early childhood was passed in an era before the First World War, a period which was still dominated for most people by the beliefs and ideals of the nineteenth century. The bulk of the professional and middle classes were orthodox upholders of religion (i.e. church-going), duty, respect for one's elders and betters, the British Empire, the sanctity of marriage and the view that sex was taboo. Certainly there were also people of more 'advanced' views, like Bernard Shaw, H. G. Wells, Havelock Ellis and others, but their influence was mainly on the younger generation, not on the over-thirties. Beckett was born into a strict Protestant family, and one may infer from the frequent references to religion in his works, and particularly those to Jesus and the Crucifixion, that religion was deeply impressed on him in those early years.

The 1914–18 war, however, brought about a tremendous upheaval in the intellectual climate of all Europe, and profoundly altered the moral and social patterns of behaviour. The intelligentsia were absorbing Einstein, Freud, Marx and Bertrand Russell in place of Newton, Darwin, Adam Smith and Herbert Spencer, and by 1926, when Beckett was a young man of twenty at Trinity College, Dublin, he and his alert contemporaries would be reading Proust and Joyce.

At Trinity College he studied French and Italian, and after taking his degree he spent two years in Paris as a 'lecteur d'anglais' at the École Normale Supérieure. In Paris he met Joyce, for whom he translated *Anna Livia Plurabelle* into French and also assisted him in preparing parts of the *Work in Progress* which became *Finnegans Wake*. Joyce and Proust were both important influences on Beckett, as also were Dante, Descartes, Schopenhauer and Berkeley. I wonder whether perhaps L. F. Celine's two novels which appeared in the thirties, *Voyage au Bout de la Nuit* and *Mort à Crédit*, may have had some slight influence too; although they are of less literary merit than Beckett's novels, and lack their profundity, they do show a very similar emotional attitude. They express powerfully the feeling of the futility and sordidness of life and that combination of disgust at bourgeois ideals and pity for the down-and-out misfits of society which Beckett shows in his *Trilogy*.

After his two years at the École and another year lecturing in French at Trinity College, and some travelling abroad and in London, Beckett finally settled down in Paris in 1937. By that time he had published a number of small pieces: a few poems; stories (*More Pricks than Kicks*); and essays (*Proust* and *Dante, Bruno, Vico, Joyce*). But these works were known to only a small circle of the *avant-garde*, and his brilliant first novel *Murphy* (published 1938) had to wait twenty years before it was republished in English, although a French translation appeared in 1947, because Beckett's name did not become widely known until the fifties after the great success of *Waiting for Godot*.

The early collection of stories, *More Pricks than Kicks*,* hinges on a prototype of the later tramps called Belacqua Shuah. His first name is derived from that slothful Florentine in Dante's *Purgatorio* who, because he left his repentance to the last moment, was condemned to spend another lifetime waiting at the foot of the hill before being permitted to climb up into Purgatory. This seems to many of Beckett's characters to be no punishment but rather the realization of their ideal of bliss—a whole lifetime resting and daydreaming in the shade of a rock without having to do anything. Belacqua is often mentioned with envy by Beckett's heroes as one who has successfully abandoned everyday life to live in a world of his own imagination.

Belacqua Shuah is such an one, a youngish man who opts out of middle-class civilized behaviour; he is an odd character who shuns company, fights shy of physical love but enjoys being a Peeping Tom. Shabby in appearance he walks like a catatonic and reveals that his heart is in the local lunatic asylum. Very significant also is his expressed desire to revert back to the caul and the darkness—a phantasy of the return to the womb which recurs with other characters. Belacqua Shuah is Beckett's first portrait of a schizoidal type which is developed more fully in *Murphy*.

These early stories, and indeed the early poems and essays,

---

* Beckett will not allow this book to be reprinted, and I have not been able to find a copy. However, Mr Fletcher deals with it in Chapter One of his *The Novels of Samuel Beckett*.

suffer somewhat from a display of erudite allusions and pedantry which suggest the highly intelligent undergraduate rather than the mature genius.

During the Second World War Beckett was in France and although, as an Irishman, he was officially a neutral he helped the Resistance movement and had to move to the Rhône Valley to escape the Gestapo.

In the country he worked on a farm, and during those war years he wrote his second novel, *Watt*. This retains a strong comic flavour, but it is more sombre and philosophical than *Murphy*. In 1945 he returned to his flat in Paris and spent the next five years writing masterpieces in French: the three novels of the *Trilogy* and *En attendant Godot*, which were published in French during 1950 to 1953 and in English from 1953 to 1956.

It is noticeable that the works which he wrote originally in French (including the late one, *Comment C'est*) are much darker, more pessimistic, and more filled with disgust at life, than are the ones written in English; the latter have a far stronger element of comedy or farce, even when, as in the later plays *All That Fall* and *Happy Days*, the whole situation is profoundly tragic.

As schizophrenia is such an important characteristic of Beckett's heroes it is advisable to discuss the main features of it here. The essential element is a withdrawal of interest from the outside world and a concentration upon an inner world of phantasy, but there are many concomitant symptoms and variations in the degree of the malady. In the catatonic form of the disease the patient is at times quite inert and seems in a stupor, while at other times he makes extraordinary gestures or takes up bizarre postures, or behaves in obviously maniacal ways, perhaps attempting suicide or homicide. Paranoic patients suffer from delusions of persecution or grandeur, hear inner voices and sometimes have visual hallucinations. The distinction between catatonic and paranoiac forms is perhaps rather one of clinical convenience than anything fundamental, since as the malady progresses it tends to include some symptoms of both types.

But there is one important and general feature, namely the poverty of the patient's emotional life; he seems to have no affection for anyone, and this trait is usually shown quite early in the course of the psychosis, or even before it is established. The patient, in Freudian terminology, has withdrawn his libido from

B

people to concentrate it narcissistically on his own ego. This feature is characteristic of the Beckett 'heroes'.

The experts differ in their views as to the cause of schizophrenia, some attributing it to bio-chemical changes, toxins in the brain, etc., while others hold that psychological and social influences are all-important. Many would agree that both physical and mental causes operate together in any actual case. It does seem that one such partial-cause which is frequently present is a disharmony in the child's relationship with a parent, usually with the mother. Frequently the child who later on develops schizophrenia had a mother who was over-possessive, domineering, and either rather hostile or apt to exploit for her own advantage the emotional mother-child relationship. An uneasy situation in which the child really fears or resents the mother, while she dislikes him, but both express their assumed affection verbally, eventually destroys the child's confidence in human relationships, and leads him to withdraw into himself and to avoid social contacts. Thus he is predisposed to escape into narcissistic phantasy. Hints of this situation in the childhood of the protagonists are given in various places in the novels.

A schizoidal condition seems to arise because a child has failed to achieve a sufficiently firm and definite sense of his own separate identity; being thus unsure of himself he fears that his personal individuality is liable to be swamped by the influences from parents, teachers and the society in which he lives, all of whom attempt to modify his personality in accordance with some approved pattern. This inevitable social pressure may be too much for a child who is not yet sure of his own personality.

To counter this threat the schizoidal type divides his ego into two selves, each necessarily incomplete and inadequate to direct and control his instincts. On the one hand he forms an *inner self* which he withdraws from contact with the outer world so that he may create his own world of phantasy with it; he concentrates his love on this inner self and regards it as the real 'me'.

On the other hand he builds up a *false self* with part of his ego in order to deal with external reality. This false self has little real feeling but it directs his bodily perceptions and movements and enables him to conform more or less to external demands and to cope, even though inadequately, with daily life.

We all are apt to go a little way along this path, shielding a small part of ourselves from exposure to the outer world, and to that extent our outer egos are not quite whole. But the schizoid withdraws a considerable part of his ego, thus leaving a manifestly depleted one with which to confront the world. And if the process goes on further it results in a definitely schizophrenic state which may end in a complete disintegration of the person. This also leads to a physical decay because the restricted false self, which has control over the bodily functions, is feeble and totally inadequate. Hence the weak eyes, stomach cramps, painful stiff legs, and eventual loss of limbs which characterize Beckett's heroes.

One of the commonest symptoms of schizophrenia is the disorder of the patient's thoughts and speech. His train of thought is liable to be broken up by the irruption of irrelevant ideas, and so his speech may consist of a series of incomplete sentences, inconsequent phrases and unrelated words. Although some patients may reason acutely and coherently, albeit often from fantastic premises, others may put forward the most outrageous *non-sequiturs*. Another disorder-trait is the compulsion to negate immediately any positive statement the patient makes; as soon as one portion of the split psyche affirms anything the other portion must contradict it. Examples of all these disorders of thought occur throughout the Beckett novels.

Beckett's interest in schizophrenia, which seems unaccountably to have been unnoticed by previous commentators, may stem from several roots, but we know of at least two opportunities which he had of observing something at first hand. When living in London (1933–5) he visited the Bethlem Royal Hospital with a doctor friend who worked there; presumably this visit arose because he was already interested in psychotics, and doubtless he learned much both from observation and from discussion with the doctor.

More important than this, however, must have been his earlier acquaintance with the Joyce family whom he saw frequently during his stay in Paris, 1929–32. We learn from Ellmann's great biography of James Joyce that the daughter, Lucia, fell rather violently in love with Beckett, who did not return her passion but had to tell her that his visits were not on her account but for the interest he had in Joyce and his work.

Now Lucia, who was talented in music, dancing, and painting, had seemed even in her teens to be odd and rather unbalanced, and in her early twenties she became noticeably less controlled. One day in 1932 (aged twenty-five) she attacked her mother in an obviously psychotic outburst, and had to be put into a sanatorium for a few days. Not very long after this she fell into a catatonic stupor and was diagnosed as a schizophrenic case. From then on

she was constantly under treatment, in and out of various sana-
toria, in the care of various doctors (including Jung, who seemed
initially to be on the way to success with her but finally failed to
effect a cure). It is hardly surprising that Beckett should have become interested in the symptoms of schizophrenia, nor that his
first novel should have a schizoidal hero who chooses to serve in
a mental home, and that his next novel should deal with the
phantasies of a schizophrenic.

# One

# 'The Seedy Solipsist'

BECKETT'S FIRST NOVEL, *Murphy*, published in 1938, is a comic masterpiece which can be enjoyed as a hilarious romp with a bunch of fantastic characters; but in fact it is also a kind of preview of all Beckett's later work, introducing almost all the main themes of the subsequent novels and plays, Murphy himself being the prototype of Watt, Moran, Molloy, and Malone. Although the treatment is highly comic, often even grotesque, the underlying themes are deeply serious and philosophical, the main ones being the nature of the relationship between the mind and the external world (which includes the body); the fundamental irrationality of reality; and the search for one's underlying true self.

In style this first novel is very different from the later ones, being written in traditional form with the author as narrator who describes and comments on the action and reports the conversations. The content, however, is far from that of any ordinary novel, and an unwary reader, beguiled by the comedy of words and situations, may easily miss many significant phrases, more especially as much of the thought is expressed either allusively or elliptically.

Murphy, formerly a theological student, then a pupil of an occultist called Neary, has come to London from Ireland to escape from his fiancée, Miss Counihan, and is installed in a room with a prostitute named Celia. He is a solipsist and his chief pleasure is to exclude the outside world and attain the bliss of living in his own mind. He does not like the noises in the street— 'They detained him in the world to which they belonged, but not he, as he fondly hoped.' Sitting naked and bound in a rocking-chair and fixing his gaze on a bright patch on the cornice moulding he hypnotizes himself so that, his body being appeased, he comes alive in his mind and dwells in a region of pure phantasy.

Celia, of course, is part of the external world from which Murphy tries to escape. But though he hates her with the part of himself that he loves, yet he loves her with the part of himself that he hates, namely his body. But we have already learnt from Neary that Murphy is incapable of romantic love.

This conflict between his narcissistic ideal ego and his mundane sensual ego naturally engenders trouble. He could manage to live by himself, owing to an amicable arrangement by which his land-lady hands him grossly exaggerated bills which a philanthropic uncle pays, so that after deducting her commission there is a wel-come balance for Murphy. But this would not be enough to sup-port Celia as well, and she, knowing how much he needs her, is determined that he shall earn enough for both of them.

Naturally, with his solipsistic outlook and his loathing for any traffic with the external world, Murphy refuses; they quarrel, and Celia departs. But now Murphy gives in, and she returns when he agrees to try to find some job. For his guidance she obtains his horoscope from an Indian Swami, and this precious document, which plays an important part later on, provides him with in-numerable reasons for not taking on this or that particular job.

Let us leave Murphy for a moment to turn to some of the supporting cast. In his farewell to Murphy, Neary 'came out of one of his dead sleeps and said: Murphy, all life is figure and ground.'

This cryptic utterance is significant in spite of its apparent irrelevance. By 'ground' Neary means the chaos of total reality, which appears to him as 'the big blooming buzzing confusion'; and by 'figure' he means the intelligible forms which he can dis-cern in it—and at the moment that means the face of Miss Dwyer. Forty pages later we read that Miss Dwyer had become 'one with the ground against which she had figured so prettily', i.e. Neary had got tired of her, and had relegated her back to the unintelli-gible chaos. A further reference occurs near the end of the story where it has a psychological significance.

It is Neary too who first introduces the theme of irrational numbers which persists throughout the novels, with his reference to Hippasos who divulged the Pythagorean mystery of the in-commensurability of the side and diagonal of a square. The square root of two, the decimal values of $\pi$ and one-seventh, and surds in general fascinate Beckett's main characters because they reveal an essentially irrational element in the universe, their exact values never being attainable, though lying between infinitely close rational limits.

Neary, having repulsed Miss Dwyer, has now transferred his attentions to Miss Counihan, who, however, is still waiting to hear from Murphy that he has made a fortune and will return to claim her hand. But no news comes, except a rumour that he had been seen lying on the grass in Hyde Park.

Eventually Neary, Wylie, Miss Counihan and one Cooper (whom they employ to trace Murphy) all go to London to find out what Murphy is doing, and whether Miss Counihan is to claim him, or marry Neary instead. The conversation of these characters provides many comic and often recondite jokes. For instance, Wylie's 'The horse leech's daughter is a closed system. Her quantum of wantum cannot vary.' The reference is to Proverbs xxx—'The horse leech has two daughters crying "Give! Give!".' As fast as one want is satisfied another arises.

To return to the main narrative, Murphy and Celia have moved to another room, whose landlady is not so obliging in the matter of crooked accounts, so that Murphy has to placate Celia by at least pretending to look for work. Every day he sets out, but 'is content to expose himself vaguely in aloof able-bodied postures on the fringes of the better slave markets,' and promptly at 6 p.m. he returns to Celia having successfully avoided any employment. Very similarly Bernard Shaw tells us how he sponged on his mother and avoided uncongenial employment. In his preface to *Immaturity* he writes:

'I dodged every opening instinctively—I was an incorrigible Unemployable, I kept up pretences (to myself as much as to others) for some time, I answered advertisements not too offensively.'

On one of these work-dodging days, sitting in a café after his fourpenny lunch, during which, by a brilliant strategem, he has managed to drink 1.83 cups of tea for the price of one, Murphy meets a dissatisfied male nurse named Ticklepenny, who wishes to leave the mental home where he works but does not want to sacrifice his month's pay by leaving too soon. Mindful of the horoscope, which mentioned both his aptitude as a custodian and the power of his eye to quell a lunatic, Murphy agrees to take over the work, leaving Ticklepenny nominally in charge so as not to forfeit his month's wage. This being settled he goes to the Park to eat his five assorted biscuits, and indulges in a nice calculation of the possible permutations, concluding that if he managed to eat them systematically in a different order each day there would be as many as one hundred and twenty separate ways of eating his meal. We shall find the same obsession with permutations in *Watt* and *Molloy*.

Chapter six is given up to an analysis of Murphy's view of his own mind, and is of considerable importance. He pictured it as a hollow sphere, hermetically sealed off from the external universe, but containing within itself, either virtually or actually, everything in the universe. He regarded the physical fact and the mental fact as equally real, though quite independent of each other, and accepted that physical facts were mysteriously paralleled by mental facts, though there were also mental facts without physical parallel. He distinguished between the 'actual' part of his mind which cognized that of which he had both mental and physical experience, and the 'virtual' part of his mind which contained that of which he had mental experience only. The actual part was light and the virtual part dark and there was a half-light part between them.

In the ordinary waking state of daily life he could think and know 'with a kind of *tic douloureux* sufficient for his parody of rational behaviour. But that was not what he understood by consciousness.' When he could rock his body to quiescence he came alive in his mind and exploited its resources. The light zone (which had forms with physical parallels) was a realm of phantasy in which the pleasure consisted in reversing his physical experience, rearranging its elements and mentally returning the blows he had endured in real life. In this 'radiant abstract of a dog's life . . . the whole physical fiasco became a howling success.' In a word, this was a state of compensatory day-dreaming.

The zone of half-light was one of contemplation and beatitude, reminiscent of Blake's state *Beulah*, 'a pleasant lovely shadow, where no dispute can come.' In it there were no physical parallels so nothing had to be put right. Psychologically this seems akin to the hypnagogic state where thought has ceased but disconnected visual images float before one's closed eyes, for though such images may have some physical parallels they do not always have them, but are usually vague and fleeting products of phantasy.

In the first two zones Murphy is still himself but in the third, the dark, he loses his sense of personal identity. This third, dark state grows more and more attractive to him so that he devotes less time to revengeful daydreams in the light, and to blissful contemplation in the half-light, and more to the dark impersonal, will-less zone where he almost ceases to be Murphy but becomes a part of nothingness. Beckett's later characters, Malone and the Unnamable, are also occupied with reaching this non-personal self which is both nothing and yet infinite, but their attitude is ambivalent since they both yearn for it and yet defend themselves against it with their continuous flow of words and stories which serve to perpetuate their disintegrating egos.

Murphy's mind being what it was, he naturally felt at home with the patients in the asylum who seemed to him to have achieved what he sought, a permanent indifference to the outer world and complete immersion in the dark zone. Of course the hospital treatment, designed to lead the patients back to normality, was anathema to him 'whose experience as a physical and rational being obliged him to call sanctuary what the psychiatrists called exile and to think of the patients not as banished from a system of benefits but as escaped from a colossal fiasco.'

If we allow for some degree of exaggeration we find that Murphy's opinion that the psychotic has escaped from a normality which is a 'colossal fiasco' anticipated by about twenty years the views of a number of modern psychiatrists who interpret the behaviour of the schizophrenic as being an attempt on his part to break out of an intolerable web of equivocal relationships existing between him and his family (or social group) which is destroying him as an autonomous person. These psychiatrists hold that our society is 'normal' only in a statistical, not a psychological sense and that the destined schizophrenic may be intrinsically saner than those who avoid actual breakdown. Normal behaviour is that to which most of us have been conditioned by our parents, teachers and social groups, and the process involves some degree of repression, introjection and mental distortion, intended for our good but frequently in fact harmful. Most people conform and survive, though their personalities have been curtailed and distorted in some measure; but many feel themselves to be invalidated by the mutually contradictory demands made on them and the unresolvable conflicts which arise therefrom. For example, a mother may make it perfectly clear to her son that she would be broken-hearted if ever he left her, but also may tell him how happy she would be if he met the right girl and married. If he is not brute enough to rebel, nor saint enough to submit, he can only escape from the impasse through a mental breakdown. In his *Psychiatry and Anti-Psychiatry* Dr Cooper puts it thus: 'Madness, that is to say, is not in a *person* but in a *system of relationships* in which the labelled patient participates. Schizophrenia, if it means anything, is a more or less characteristic mode of disturbed group behaviour.' Murphy was right to reject our 'normality', which is largely a system of false relationships; his error was in believing that the psychotic had achieved the true sanity of an autonomous self who is equally at home in both the inner and outer reality.

In spite of his oddity, his anti-social disposition, and his attraction for the irrational and the infinite, Murphy is not actually insane. He does not suffer from hallucinations nor from delusions of grandeur or of persecution, nor does he hear inner voices; and he is quite capable of orienting himself in the world and managing his own affairs. But he is acutely aware of the difference between what he calls 'the big world' outside and the 'little world' of his mind in which he can love himself in freedom. He chooses the latter deliberately, consciously, and quite rationally, and rejects the 'colossal fiasco' outside.

When he goes to take up his duties at the mental home he does not tell Celia what the job is, nor where it is, but abandons her quite simply; and shortly afterwards returns while she is out and collects his precious rocking chair, having decided to make the break final. He has fixed up a gas stove in a garret, connected precariously with the disused gas jet in a lavatory on the floor below, and now with his rocking chair and sagging bed, in the thick fug, he feels almost as well off as the privileged inmates of the padded cells which 'surpassed by far all he had even been able to imagine in the way of indoor bowers of bliss.'

Murphy is most attracted by the gentle schizophrenic Mr Endon, with whom he plays chess, making his moves in the intervals between his duties, so that a game lasted all day or all night; and often neither player would lose a piece or check the other, for this game was a kind of non-chess. One night, at the end of a game, Murphy suffers what is evidently a preliminary attack foreshadowing the schizophrenia for which he would seem destined. He sees Mr Endon in a vivid blur of brilliantly coloured glitter as 'Neary's big blooming buzzing confusion or ground, mercifully free of figure.' This lasts only a short time, the vision fades and he sees nothing, while his other senses are also in abeyance and he feels immersed in 'the accidentless One-and-Only, conveniently called Nothing.' On waking from this fit he discovers that Mr Endon has escaped from the cell and is enjoying himself by switching on and off all the lights in the various cells. Murphy rescues him and tucks him up in bed and stares into his eyes, and for the first time hears an inner voice dictating words to him, to the effect that the last he saw of Mr Endon was his own face reflected in Mr Endon's eyes. This initial attack is actually the second hint we have been given of the probable oncoming of schizophrenia. While Murphy

was rocking in his garret on a previous night Ticklepenny observed that he had a great look of one Clarke, who had been in a
catatonic stupor for three weeks, and Ticklepenny warned
Murphy to look out—but Murphy was highly gratified to find
that he had actually looked like such an advanced Schizo.

Leaving the cell Murphy goes out into the garden, takes off his
clothes, lies down on the wet grass and tries to visualize Celia,
then his mother, then in turn all his acquaintances, but in vain.
Only fragments of forms will appear, and he senses the danger of
persisting and reaching deeper and darker levels. In fact for the
first time he approaches the really frightening depth of the psyche
where he would not be 'a mote in the absolute freedom' but a
nothingness; a region of horror, darkness and void often experienced by mystics, whether Christian or Oriental. So he pulls himself together, and returns to his garret, lights the candle (but not
the gas fire) and gets into the rocking-chair intending to soothe
himself for a short time in the familiar zones in which he felt free,
and afterwards to dress and return to Celia, leaving Ticklepenny
to cope with the asylum duties. Clearly his recent experience in
Mr Endon's cell was a terrifying glimpse of an abyss below the
dark zone which he had courted, a state in which he would be
non-Murphy.

Alas, while he is rocking, appeased and almost shut off from
externals, some one down below pulls the chain of the gas jet. Gas
pours out of the unlit fire, and Murphy dies. In the explosion
which is caused by the lighted candle, his body is charred; and its
subsequent identification by Celia, the cremation which is attended
by the quartet from Ireland whose search is thus ended, and the
disposal of his ashes, provide comic material for the next chapter.
Finally, Celia returns to her grandfather, Mr Kelly, and resumes
the profession which she had hoped to abandon in favour of life
with Murphy. And so this grotesque chronicle ends, on a quiet,
vaguely sad note, with the implied death of Mr Kelly—a very
minor character in this tale, but noteworthy as being the first of
that series of old men who were to occupy the major place in
Beckett's later works.

# Two

# 'A Matrix of Surds'

IN 1942 BECKETT WROTE the French translation of *Murphy*, which was published five years later, and during the years 1942 to 1947 he was writing *Watt* in English, although it was not published until 1953 after the success of *Waiting for Godot* had brought him fame. This second novel has great affinities with the first, most of whose themes are here developed more fully, Watt himself being the schizophrenic that Murphy was about to become when the gas ended his life. But Beckett hints at the essential identity of Watt and Murphy when the former refers to 'constellations which he had once known familiarly by name when dying in London.' Other authors have been known to resuscitate a character whom they had unfortunately killed off before they had really finished with him, and Beckett, who had a lot more to say about Murphy, discreetly just gives him a new name—a manoeuvre which he uses with even greater justification in the later Trilogy.

The novel begins in much the same mood as does *Murphy*, with comic and bawdy conversation between three characters whom we do not meet again, for there is no sub-plot in this story such as involved the Irish quartet. These three people notice Watt getting off a tram and walking towards the station, and from their discussion of him we learn that he is a mild, inoffensive man, of no fixed address, probably educated at a university, a milk drinker, truthful, a little strange at times, and that he has a large red nose; he once borrowed five shillings from one of them and has not yet been able to pay it back. Thus Watt appears to the outside public as a seedy, harmless vagabond, and his general inadequacy is illustrated when he bumps into a porter who is wheeling a milk can at the station. This incident is symbolical. At each end of the platform is a group of milk cans and the porter is engaged in wheeling the cans of the first group one by one to the other end, and those of the second group to the first end: a picture of the futile activity of mankind, incessantly moving matter but leaving things just as they always were, which makes Watt reflect on the porter's task that 'perhaps it is a punishment for disobedience, or some neglect of duty.'

This is surely an echo from Dostoevsky's *House of the Dead* in which he suggests that the really crushing punishment, which would reduce a criminal to suicide, would be to condemn him 'to pour water from one vessel into another, or to transport a quantity of earth from one place to another, in order to perform the contrary operation immediately afterwards.'

After this little contretemps he gets into a compartment which, we are told, is empty, but when the train has started we find it contains a large man named Spiro who edits a popular Catholic monthly, and mingles theology with irreverent bawdy in the manner of Buck Mulligan. A reader has posed the following query: 'A rat, or other small animal, eats of a consecrated wafer. 1) Does he ingest the Real Body, or does he not? 2) If he does not, what has become of it? 3) If he does, what is to be done with him?' Mr Spiro answers questions one and three learnedly at great length, but Watt does not hear him (nor do we) for he is listening to his inner voice, which he sometimes understood wholly, sometimes in part, and sometimes not at all.

'Personally I would pursue him, said Mr Spiro, if I were sure it was he, with all the rigour of the canon laws. He took his legs off the seat. He put his head out of the window. And pontifical decrees, he cried. A great rush of air drove him back. He was alone, flying through the night.'

Immediately after this we have a description of Watt walking with his peculiar gait along a road in the moonlight. Evidently the train stopped at the station while Spiro was saying his first sentence. Watt got out, and Spiro opened the window to shout the second part, about pontifical decrees, after him, by which time the train had started again.

Watt has an extraordinary way of walking, which is described comically at some length. He thrusts his legs out stiffly at awkward angles and twists his body, and plunges forward 'like a headlong tardigrade'. These grotesque movements (and the somewhat similar ones of Molloy in the next novel), as also his later method (in chapter three) of walking backwards, stumbling and falling, reveal him as a catatonic schizophrenic, and this is why Beckett takes the trouble to describe them so fully.

After walking a while Watt feels weak and tired so he lies down, first on the path and then in the ditch, where he listens to the voices of a choir, which seem to be really external and far away, singing as follows:

> *Fifty two point two eight five seven*
> *One four two eight five seven one four two*
> *great granma Magrew how do you do*
> *blooming thanks and you drooping thanks and you*
> *withered thanks and you forgotten thanks and you*
> *thanks forgotten too great granma Magrew.*

Professor Kenner, in his admirable study of Beckett, has dealt at some length with the significance for Beckett of non-terminating decimals such as this. They reveal an intrinsic irrationality in the universe, for we must remember that the ratio of the diagonal to the side of a square, or that of the circumference to the diameter of a circle, relate to plane geometry, the most rational and abstract of sciences, while that most irrational of all numbers, the square root of minus one, is indissolubly bound up with relativity physics. Beckett, then, uses them as symbols, but for his characters they are obsessions, part of the syndrome of their mania. The introduction of the recurring decimal at this point of the story indicates that Watt has now detached himself from the 'whole physical fiasco' of the outside world, and henceforth will experience 'the big blooming buzzing confusion or ground, mercifully free of figure.' The song ended, he resumes his walk and quickly reaches his goal, the house of Mr Knott, which is the irrational world of phantasy inside the schizophrenic's head.

From now on we lose contact with the outside world to plunge into the phantasies of Watt's mind and the lengthy ratiocinations, catalogues of possibilities and alternatives which characterize his particular form of mania. Naturally this is difficult reading, and far from what most people expect in a novel; but though there are tedious pages where one is tempted to skip over the catalogue after reading the first few items, the book is curiously gripping and full of rewards for careful readers.

I have said that Mr Knott's house is Watt's world of phantasy, but who is this master, Mr Knott, whom Watt has come to serve? He might be interpreted as God, for he moves in equally mysterious ways, but his name suggests both a knot, a nucleus in which many strands are inextricably joined, or in the words of a dic-

tionary 'the central part of a tangle', and also the negative 'not'
with which any description of Brahm must begin—not-this, not-
that. In fact Mr Knott is a personification of the central real Self,
that 'Matrix of Surds' which is at once infinite and nothing, and
which is the goal of the mystic's quest, as it is of Watt's; for Watt
may be regarded as a personification of the 'what?' which man
asks about his own existence and that of the world outside.

When Watt has seated himself in Mr Knott's kitchen the departing servant, Arsene, whom he is to replace, arrives and gives him
a lengthy and intricate account of things, from which we learn
that Mr Knott always has two servants who stay for a period, but
inevitably the senior one departs at some point, when the junior
takes his place and a stranger automatically arrives to become the
new junior. The newcomer is at peace with himself very soon,
feeling 'the sensations of imminent harmony, when all outside
him will be he . . . when in a word he will be in his midst at last,
after so many tedious years spent clinging to the perimeter . . .
what a feeling of security.'

This is Watt's version of Murphy's 'dark zone', but unfortunately it does not last, and Arsene goes on to relate how one day he
was sitting in the yard when the change occurred.

'In what did it consist? It is hard to say. Something slipped . . .
some tiny little thing. Gliss . . . iss . . . iss—STOP!'

This change, which ends the early mystical stage of harmony
and identification with the universe, he calls 'the reversed meta-
morphosis. The Laurel into Daphne. The old thing where it
always was, back again.'

Beckett is a mystic, but of an unusual type. We generally expect
the mystical experience to be one of intense joy, a union of the soul
with God or The One, which sanctifies life, or leads to a blissful
Nirvana. We associate it with the Christian saints, or Buddha, or
holy oriental sages. But in Beckett's visions we find that the
ground of our Being is a terrible abyss from which the self recoils
lest it should fall into annihilation. To other mystics (for example
St John of the Cross) this is a well-known stage which must be
passed through before true union is achieved; but Beckett's
characters do not pass beyond it.

While on this topic of mysticism we may note an illuminating
remark of Freud's which is highly relevant to Watt's mental state.
At the end of his essay on 'The Dissection of the Psychical
Personality' (*New Introductory Lectures on Psycho-Analysis*) in which
he has brought out the facts that the id is a stranger to ideas of

logic, of good and bad, and of time, and further that one function of the ego is to represent the external world to the id, and finally has warned the reader that the ego, super-ego, and id are not rigidly separated by sharp dividing lines but that the boundaries may vary and the divisions may shade into one another, he adds quite casually: 'It is easy to imagine, too, that certain mystical practices may succeed in upsetting the normal relations between the different regions of the mind, so that, for instance, perception may be able to grasp happenings in the depths of the ego and the id which were otherwise inaccessible to it. It may safely be doubted, however, whether this road will lead us to the ultimate truths from which salvation is to be expected.'

It would seem quite plausible, however, to regard the schizo-phrenic state as one in which normally inaccessible happenings in the deeper levels of the ego and the id are, if not 'grasped' in the sense of 'comprehended', at least confusedly perceived, and that this may be one source of the irrationality of the patient.

Arsene now departs, leaving Watt to take up his duties on the ground floor which the other servant, Erskine, relinquishes in order to take over from Arsene on the first floor where Mr Knott resides.

Chapter two is devoted to Watt's experience on the ground-floor where he had a few menial duties to perform, of which the most important seems to be the preparation of Mr Knott's food which is composed of every kind of meat, fish, poultry, soup, bread-butter together with numerous beverages, from water and milk to brandy and absinthe, plus many medicines for his health, all mixed and cooked together in one pot, and sufficient to last the whole week.

The first, and most important event is the arrival of two piano-tuners, the Galls, father and son. Up till now, we are told, Watt had always lived, though miserably, among face values; whatever he saw with the first look was enough, more than enough for him. But this incident quickly appeared quite meaningless to him. In Watt's mind the whole scene became a totally unintelligible interplay of visual and audible stimuli devoid of all meaning, because he had lost the faculty of correlating his sensations. But Watt 'was obliged because of his peculiar character to enquire into what they meant. Oh not into what they really meant, his character was not so peculiar as all that, but into what they might be induced to mean, with the help of a little patience, a little ingenuity.'

Watt's is a reasoning mind presented with numerous connected sensations which he must co-ordinate into some meaningful pattern, for he has lost the accepted normal pattern which sane
men automatically impose; so perhaps the incident never took
place as recorded, but 'only an unintelligible succession of changes,
from which Watt finally extracted the Galls and the piano, in self-
defence?'

After this episode Watt finds himself in a mental state in which,
when looking at a pot, he feels sure that it is not really a pot,
although it is almost a pot and for practical purposes is used as
one. And of himself he finds that he cannot affirm anything with
confidence, neither that he is a man nor that he is in the street, for
example. Then he longs for Erskine to talk to him, which would
reassure him of his own reality. In short, his perceptual system has
become aware of happenings in the deeper layers of the ego and
the id because the normal boundary between them has altered.

Both *Murphy* and *Watt* raise the old question as to the validity
of normal sense perception—are what we term the distorted or
deranged perceptions of the lunatic, or the transcendent perceptions of the mystic, delusive, or are they merely different from the
normal but equally valid? Blake's penetrating question:

*How do you know but every bird that cuts the airy way*
*Is an immense world of delight closed by your senses five?*

has never been answered. We interpret our sense-data in a coherent
way which seems to work, but what would our picture of the
external world be like if our sense of sight, for example, did not
cover the rainbow spectrum but embraced an octave of x-rays; or
if our hearing extended say ten octaves above our present highest
audible note? Doubtless we should still make a coherent interpretation, but it would be a vastly different one.

I am not, of course, suggesting that hyperaesthesia is a feature
of schizophrenia (though it has been observed in certain dis-
sociated states of hypnotic or mediumistic trance), for the reverse
is actually the case; a considerable dulling of the senses is the rule.
But it is conceivable that Watt's pot appeared in some way to be
not quite a pot because he perceived something in it which we
could not see, nor could he describe with the concepts he had
been conditioned to use. The poet Edward Carpenter in *Towards*
c

*Democracy*, referring to the effect of the mystical ecstasy, says: 'From that day forward objects turn round upon themselves with an exceedingly innocent air, but are visibly not the same.'

The idea that we impose certain forms on our perceptions and automatically select what we shall perceive of the external world is of course a familiar one. William James (in *Principles of Psychology*) uses the analogy of a sculptor who out of a block of stone extricates one particular statue though a thousand others are latent in it. 'Other sculptors, other statues! Other minds, other worlds from the same monotonous and inexpressive chaos. My world is but one in a million alike embedded, alike real to those who may abstract them.'

Since the vast majority of human beings have approximately identical mental constitutions, in that they agree in their division of the continuum into time and three-space, they all tend to abstract the same world and this naturally appears to be the only real one. But in unusual mental states there may be a different selection, with different mental forms imposed, giving another real world which cannot quite be reconciled with our normal one. It may well be that the schizophrenic extricates a somewhat different world from the chaos; not perhaps a consistent and unvarying one, but one of sufficient intensity to prevent him from coping with our normal world, so that a civilized society can only deal with him as a patient in a mental home. But the world seen by the patient may be just as valid as that seen by his doctor. Indeed it may well be that our normal 'sane' perception of external reality is in fact a distorted one, and that Blake's World of Imagination was as close to reality as Dr Johnson's common-sense.

Mr Knott had ruled that when he did not eat all of his meal the remains should be given to the dog. But there was no dog in the house. Watt resolves this difficulty in a wonderful *tour de force* lasting some twenty-six pages, in which he canvasses the possible ways of always having a famished dog brought to the house on the days when there is the food available, which involves positing the Lynch family, whose twenty-eight members are described, to provide a succession of servants to take charge of the series of dogs needed over the years. It is one of Beckett's richest comic passages.

Watt spends a lot of time speculating on Erskine's movements; on why the bell is rung in Erskine's room; on how to get into Erskine's room so as to confirm the existence of the bell; on the question of how long he would remain on the ground-floor, and on the infinite series of servants needed to attend on Mr Knott. For he is an inflexible rationalist, however bizarre his premises, and must impose meaning and order on his phantasies. When he gets into Erskine's room Watt is fascinated by a picture which hangs there. It shows a black circle on a white ground with a blue dot placed inside the circle but not at its centre. The dot and circle seem to lie in different planes and to be moving, now one, then the other receding or advancing. It appears to Watt to represent a circle searching for its true centre and a centre searching for its circumference; which is a symbol of the relationship between the mortal ego and the true self, or of that between Watt and Mr Knott. It is also symbolically important that the circle has a break at its lowest point, a gateway to the nothingness from whence the centre might enter into the circle.

In a more lucid moment he recalls the time in his past life when he flirted with Mrs Gorman the fishwoman. They used to sit alternately in each other's laps, kissing, in the kitchen, 'but further than this, it will be learnt with regret, they never went.' And he wonders what drew them together and conjectures that perhaps the smell of fish attracted him, while the bottle of stout which he provided attracted her. From this we can gather that, like Murphy, Watt was a stranger to love.

In all this time he has seen Mr Knott only rarely, and learned nothing definite about him and is now tired of the ground-floor. But one morning Erskine departs, and a strange man, named Arthur appears in the kitchen. So we hope and expect that in the next chapter Watt, having been promoted to the first floor, will be able to report on the nature and doings of his mysterious employer.

In Chapter three the narration is taken up by Sam, a lunatic to whom Watt has told his story while both of them are inmates of an asylum at some undetermined time after Watt had left Knott's home. The two madmen have achieved what Murphy aspired to, revelling 'each in his separate soundless unlit warmth' of the padded cell.

Nevertheless, they occasionally go out into the garden where they meet, and they take to one another at sight, as Murphy took to Mr Endon. Here, at various times, and with various forms of distorted language (inversions of words, or of their order in the sentence, etc.), Watt tells Sam of his life on the first floor in Mr Knott's house.

Watt's inversions of words, sentences, etc., might seem to be merely a comic touch of Beckett's, having no intrinsic significance, but in fact they are perfectly sound examples of schizophrenic speech-disorders. Apparently nonsensical sets of words, when recorded and examined (which naturally happens only occasionally) may be found to be quite coherent rational phrases or sentences either with the words displaced or pronounced backwards. Thus Dr Navratil (*Schizophrenie und Sprache*) instances a patient who greeted the doctor with the seemingly meaningless words 'Tsrarebo rehgat netug,' which was discovered, by chance, to be 'Guten Tag Herr Oberarzt' pronounced backwards. Similarly Watt begins by saying, 'Day of most, night of part, Knott with now,' then progresses from saying 'Pardon beg' to 'Geb nodrap'; and later still he says 'Ton kawa, ton pelsa' for 'Not awake, not asleep;' and 'Deen did taw? Tonk? Tog da taw? Tonk,' etc., etc.

This reversal of words or sentences is a compulsive spontaneous action on the part of the patient; it is not consciously contrived and rehearsed beforehand as is the case in the children's game of back-slang, in which fun is found in learning a rhyme such as 'Bmal elttila dah yram,' and puzzling the uninitiated with this apparently strange and secret language.

We do not learn much of Mr Knott or his doings, for apparently Watt saw and heard little of him, and in any case Watt's senses were decaying, but we gather that he was protean in nature; his limbs, features, shape, size, clothes, voice, etc., etc., varied from day to day. But there is one highly philosophical judgement about him: 'Mr Knott needing nothing if not, one, not to need, and, two, a witness to his not needing, of himself knew nothing, And so he needed to be witnessed. Not that he might know, no, but that he might not cease.' This is the reason for the series of servants, Arsene, Erskine, and Watt—they enable Mr Knott to be conscious of his own existence.

The need to be witnessed by another, a *motif* which recurs through Beckett's works, and is his formulation of the doctrine *esse est percipi*, receives curious confirmation from an unexpected quarter. The well-known medium Mrs Willett received messages purporting to come from the deceased F. W. H. Myers and Edmund Gurney, and these two 'spirits' said they often had great difficulty in retaining their own sense of personal identity while they were communicating via the medium's mind and body, and they added that it was only *her* awareness of them that enabled them to remain aware of themselves as separate persons.

Sam describes how he and Watt divert themselves in the garden by wantonly killing birds, by making friends with rats and feeding them live fledglings or frogs, and as a super refinement of maniacal sadism 'seizing suddenly a plump young rat, resting in our bosom after its repast, we would feed it to its mother, or its father or its brother, or its sister, or to some less fortunate relative. It was on these occasions we agreed, after an exchange of views, that we came nearest to God.'

This horrible paragraph, with its bitter conclusion, is not only true to the psychology of certain types of mania, in which a defeated ego achieves through wanton cruelty or murder a phantasy of God-like omnipotence; it is also, by implication, a commentary on the essential evil of power, whether the omnipotence of Jehovah who sent the flood, destroyed the cities of the plain, and afflicted Egypt with the plagues; or human power which results in oriental tyrannies, Spanish Inquisitions, Russian pogroms, secret police, the S.S. and Hitler's extermination of the Jews.

The chapter contains a long digression lasting twenty-eight pages consisting of a story about an old peasant who extracts cube-roots in his head, and is brought by Mr Louit to a committee of investigators. The story seems to have no relevance to Watt but to be an excuse for some comedy and for an analysis of the number of possible ways the five members of the committee can each look at each of the others.

After this long digression we return to the information which Watt was giving Sam about Mr Knott, his singing, his appearance, his manner of dressing and of putting on his boots or slippers, none of which of course, enables us to form any valid picture of the 'unthinkable unspeakable' which Mr Knott symbolizes. And finally Sam describes Watt retreating backwards, through the hole in a fence, stumbling and falling, back to the pavilion where he now dwelt separated from Sam, who never saw him again after this.

Chapter four goes back to the night when Watt departed from Mr Knott's house. We are never told how long he had been either on the ground floor or on the first floor, nor what time elapsed before he entered the asylum, for, as Freud pointed out, the id knows nothing of time. But we did learn, in chapter three, that his senses had decayed, that he reached a state of apathy in which the house, the garden and Arthur were completely indifferent for him, so that on his departure he went out with the utmost serenity.

That night he finds a stranger, named Micks, in the kitchen, so he gathers up his two bags and, wrapped up in his greatcoat and with his old pepper-coloured block hat on his head, he sets out for the railway station.

On his arrival there his attention is arrested by a strange figure walking down the road. He cannot tell if it is man or woman, priest or nun. It is apparently clothed in a single garment which might have been a sheet, sack, quilt or rug, and on its head sits 'the likeness of a depressed inverted chamber-pot, yellow with age, to put it politely.'

This apparition walks with a peculiar gait, splaying out its feet widely, and never advancing any nearer although it has been plunging forward for perhaps half an hour. And then it fades away, leaving Watt puzzled and fascinated.

This peculiar apparition corresponds closely with Watt's first appearance in the book, when the onlookers saw him get down from the tram and Mr Hackett 'was not sure that it was not a parcel, a carpet for example, or a roll of tarpaulin.' Watt remained at the tram-stop perfectly motionless for a time before moving off to the station; and we know already about his peculiar method of walking which was described in the first chapter. It seems obvious that these detailed correspondences are there to indicate that Watt was seeing his double (as Maupassant once did), which is a known, though uncommon, hallucination to which split personalities are liable.

The station is closed, with everything locked up, so Watt goes to the signal-box and induces the signalman to unlock the waiting-room and let him spend the night there, and the cautious signalman locks him in.

In the early morning the porter arrives to unlock all the doors, which he does with gusto, banging them open with a violent kick, and incidentally knocking Watt down, stunned, to the floor. The stationmaster and some travellers arrive, and Watt is brought round with a bucket of water.

Finally he buys a ticket to the end of the line, but does not take either the 5.55 train or the 6.4, but walks out of the station, presumably to be picked up and committed to the asylum.

So ends this strange tale in which the comic vision which pervaded Murphy is now mingled with a bitter feeling of the horror that is built into the universe, and a vivid sense of the indignities of human physiology, comparable to what we find in portions of Shakespeare and Swift. And who but Beckett could have successfully created out of the irrational phantasies of a madman an intelligible and intriguing novel in which the interest lies not in violent action or a tragic situation such as a Poe or a Maupassant might depict but in the disordered mental life itself? For the account of Watt's stay in Mr Knott's house in fact reproduces the subjective experience of a schizophrenic.

We may distinguish at least four stages in Watt's psychosis. The initial one which lasts until the point where he hears the anthem of a recurring decimal; then his sojourn on the ground floor at Mr Knott's; thirdly his service on the first floor, which is reported indirectly via his lunatic friend Sam; and lastly his final stay in an asylum, after his discharge from Knott's house. This fourth stage is revealed by Sam's account of Watt's behaviour, manner of movement, and disordered modes of speech. It is evidently one of even greater disintegration than the others.

# The Trilogy

## MOLLOY
## MALONE DIES
## THE UNNAMABLE

*Who may tell the tale*
*of the old man?*
*weigh absence in a scale?*
*mete want with a span?*
*the sum assess*
*of the world's woes?*
*nothingness*
*in words enclose?*

(from Addenda to *Watt*)

# *Three*

# 'A Wandering to Find Home'

In 1946, after having written *Watt*, Beckett wrote (in French) the *Three Stories* dealing with an old outcast. These were published in France in 1955, but the English translation appeared only in 1967 in the volume of short prose pieces called *No's Knife*. The three stories are Beckett's preliminary delineation of the schizoidal old tramp who was later portrayed at much greater length in the three novels of *The Trilogy*, where the themes are developed with considerably more detail, so that it would be tedious to enlarge on them here.

In the first story, *The Expelled*, the tramp is thrown out into the street and wanders round the town, at first on foot and then in a cab in which he also spends the night parked in the cabman's stable. The second story, *The Calmative*, begins with his assertion that he was about ninety years old when he died; but he is only dead in the sense that he has lost his sense of individual identity and of reality.

After sundry wanderings through a wood and the town and by the seashore he meets a man who, in exchange for a kiss, gives him a phial containing some tranquilizing drug. Then he wanders on through the town until he collapses in the street, but recovers and continues his hopeless journey.

The third story, *The End*, is the most interesting of the three. Discharged from some hospital or asylum the old man wanders once more through the city, and eventually finds a lodging from which, however, he is soon evicted by the landlord. After roaming the countryside and sharing a cave by the sea with another derelict he goes to a shed on a mountain for a while. Soon, nearly starving, he returns to the city where he supports himself by begging and lives in an abandoned shed by the riverside.

This shed contains an old boat in which he sleeps, and his story ends with an hallucinatory vision of himself floating down the river, opening a hole in the bottom of the boat, swallowing his calmative and lying down comfortably to drown. But this is a suicide in phantasy, not in reality—indeed, how could he ever have launched the boat?—for he lives 'without the courage to end, or the strength to go on.'

These *Three Stories* evidently unleashed a whole flood of ideas in Beckett's mind, for the next years, 1947 to 1949, were intensely creative and in them he wrote four extraordinary masterpieces, *Molloy, Malone Dies, The Unnamable* and *Waiting for Godot.*

# Molloy

The first book of the *Trilogy* is divided into two apparently disconnected parts, the first dealing with Molloy and the second with another character called Moran. But the similarities between these two men, and the parallelism in their respective adventures, both physical and mental, lead one to conclude that they are actually the same person, Moran being the middle-aged Molloy. In fact the *Trilogy* is one continuous whole in which the ostensibly different characters—Molloy, Moran, Malone, Sapo, Macmann, Mahood—are all the personae of the same essential self, the Unnamable.

The import of *Molloy* becomes clearer if we read Part Two first, since the story of Moran precedes and elucidates that of Molloy.

When we first meet Moran he is apparently a reasonably well-to-do widower of about fifty with a teen-age son whom he treats abominably, though justifying his arbitrary severity with high moral principles. His relationship with his son is a mixture of rather mawkish sentiment with a strong sadistic pleasure in domineering over him. He constantly suspects the boy of deception and disobedience, and he disciplines him unmercifully, ostensibly for the boy's own good, of course, but really because he delights in maintaining his authority as a father. His is a mean and restricted personality, solitary by choice because he is timid amongst other men, meticulous, punctual, parsimonious and obstinate. He is, in fact, what Freud designated as an anal character; and it is surely not accidental that his home town is named Turdy.

He is seated in the garden one Sunday morning during the summer holidays, happily doing nothing, when a man named Gaber approaches with instructions from his chief, one Youdi. Moran is told to set out with his son that day in search of Molloy

—though he is not told what to do when he has found him. He is annoyed, but sends Gaber to the kitchen to get himself a glass of beer. After reflecting that he has now missed Mass he goes to the kitchen and finds to his surprise that Gaber never went there but has evidently quietly vanished.

After considering the question of whether he shall set out on his autocycle, then calling on the priest to receive the communion, and nagging at his son, he decides to rest awhile in his bed. We find his view of life is fundamentally that of Murphy and Watt. Lying down in the warmth he finds peace in a darkness where formless masses move; but when he gets up and goes out everything changes: '. . . the noise of things bursting, merging, avoiding one another assails me on all sides, my eyes search in vain for two things alike, each pinpoint of skin screams a different message. I drown in the spray of phenomena.' It is the 'big blooming buzzing confusion' again.

Although Moran has never been told about Molloy, or seen him, yet he knows something of him: 'Molloy, or Mollose, was no stranger to me. . . . Perhaps I had invented him, I mean found him ready-made in my head.' Molloy, in fact, is really a persona towards which Moran's disintegrating self is striving, for it is by now clear that Moran is not wholly sane.

'He (Molloy) panted. He had only to rise up within me for me to be filled with panting . . . he was massive and hulking . . . forever on the move. This was how he came to me, at long intervals. Then I was nothing but uproar, bulk, rage, suffocation, effort unceasing, frenzied and vain. Just the opposite of myself, in fact.'

Just so, one may imagine, does the fitful and gradual formation of a secondary personality seem to the primary one which it seeks to displace. *The Trilogy* indeed may be regarded as the tale of a multiple personality of a somewhat unorthodox sort, since Beckett's series of vagabonds are all variants of the attempt to form one satisfactory 'little ego' out of one and the same 'big id'.

And it is not only Molloy that Moran knows: 'What a rabble in my head, what a gallery of moribunds. Murphy, Watt, Yerk, Mercier and all the others.'

Gaber is not on the same plane as these personae; he is an hallucination, a projection of Moran's Super-ego, Youdi, the chief whose commands have to be obeyed. Gaber's nature is betrayed both by his mysterious disappearance without having gone to the kitchen for his beer, and by his sudden inexplicable appearance (and also his vanishing) to Moran at a later stage of the story.

Moran himself in moments of lucidity 'came even to doubt the existence of Gaber himself . . . and I might have gone to the extreme of conjuring away the chief too and regarding myself as solely responsible for my wretched existence.' But he dare not deny the reality of Youdi, for that would lead him to suicide and he is not strong enough for that. It is Youdi's voice he listens to, the inner voice which 'is rather an ambiguous voice and not always easy to follow, in its reasonings and decrees. But I follow it none the less more or less.'

During the first forty pages of the story, Moran is by no means wholly divorced from reality, in spite of the indications of unbalance which I mentioned. He is concerned with visiting his priest, his household arrangements, his garden, bees and hens, and very much with the behaviour of his son, whom he thwarts and ill-treats while constantly feeling that the boy is always trying to defy him. For example, the lad would like to take a few of his treasured stamps with him on their expedition; but Moran removes the albums on the ground that it will teach him life's most valuable lesson—how to do without. Naturally aggrieved, the boy sulks and cries in his room.

At nine o'clock 'the sound of a gong, struck with violence' summons Moran to his evening meal. This gong appears again, for in Part One, when Molloy is crawling through the forest, he repeatedly hears the sound of a gong, inexplicable in that place. It is of course an auditory hallucination and quite understandable as such in a man who formerly owned a gong. One further detail of significance later on emerges when Moran tells us that as a rule he sat down to table in good time and played with the knife-rest while waiting to be served.

Tonight the meal is not a success, for the soup is cold, the shepherd's pie uneatable, and the boy sulky and feverish. Moran gives his son some milk and sends him to bed for an hour or two; then, feeling depressed, he takes a turn in the garden before going in to prepare for the journey. He puts on a shooting-suit with knee-breeches and stockings, a pair of shiny black boots, a yellow straw boater held under the chin with an elastic band; a get-up which is 'an example of well-bred bad taste'. In addition, he chooses a heavy umbrella, rather than wearing a cape.

When at last it is time to start he goes to his son's room to find him sleeping heavily. He shakes the boy and struggles to get him up, but the lad resists and finally, when dragged out he rolls on the floor, 'screaming with anger and defiance'. This throws

Moran into a maniacal fit of rage in which he thrashes the boy with his stout umbrella, held 'by the end with both hands'. Recognizing that in his rage he might murder his son ('I hear . . . the benches creaking in the court of assizes') he drops the umbrella and rushes down to the shed outside, seizes an axe and hacks madly at a chopping block. This done, he returns quite calmed and helps his weeping son to dress, just as if nothing had happened.

Ever since Gaber's visit Moran's behaviour has been peculiar and often irrational, but this is the first definitely psychotic incident, and it reveals how near the Molloy personality is now to the surface. This personality is of course antithetical to Moran's; it is uncontrolled, impulsive and purely instinctual. The Molloy country is described in terms which recall the metaphorical park in *Venus and Adonis*. Its name is Ballyba and it is bounded by smiling, undulating land which encloses pasture, bogland, copses and a narrow tidal creek.

Eventually, at midnight Moran sets out, followed by his stumbling son, on what is clearly a psychological as well as a geographical journey—in fact a 'fugue'. They walk on for several days, living on tinned food and building shelters with branches or sleeping in the open and Moran spends much time wondering what Gaber meant him to do with Molloy when he found him. Then one night he wakes with a violent pain in one knee, and his leg goes stiff so that he cannot bend it—this is the first step in the progressive physical deterioration that accompanies his transformation into Molloy. In order to be able to continue his journey he sends his son off to the nearest town to buy a bicycle, and during the days before the bicycle arrives he wanders about a little with the help of his umbrella. Two curious incidents occur at this period. First he sees a man standing holding a stick that was more like a club. The man had snow-white hair, and wore an extraordinary hat and a coat much too heavy for the time of year. This man asked for bread and when given a piece broke it into two and put it in his pocket, after which he walked away. One guesses from the scanty details that this might be an externalization of the Molloy persona which is struggling to oust the Moran one.

The second incident occurs on another evening, when a stranger accosts him, enquiring if he has seen an old man with a stick pass by. The odd thing was that this stranger's face, 'I regret to say, vaguely resembled my own, less the refinement of course, same little abortive moustache, same little ferrety eyes. . . .' So he appears to be an hallucination of Moran's 'Double'; and this fits

with the immediately following incident, for Moran sees the man's
hand coming to clutch him, and 'I do not know what happened
then. But a little later, perhaps a long time later, I found him
stretched on the ground his head in a pulp. I am sorry I cannot
indicate more clearly how this result was obtained, it would have
been something worth reading.' (Note the emotional incongruity
of the last sentence!) And after this comes the important statement 'He no longer resembled me.'

We can interpret this as a pure hallucination, the whole murder
and subsequent description of how he disposed of the body and
hunted for his scattered keys, dragging himself forward cata-
tonically clutching the grass and rolling over and over, being
enacted in phantasy. Or we may believe that an actual man was
really attacked by the maniac who projected on to him his own
features. In either case the important point is the initial identification of the man with the Moran personality which the emerging
Molloy personality was trying to supplant. At the moment of the
attack Moran suffered a black-out, for at that moment Molloy
had gained control. This manic fit, whose ferocity is emphasized
by the fact that Moran found a torn-off ear on the ground, marks
the point where Molloy really gains the upper hand for a while,
though he keeps it only temporarily.

When this fit has subsided the boy returns with a bicycle, and
they continue their journey, during which they have to overcome
many obstacles and circumvent many fiends before arriving in the
Molloy country, Ballyba.

Seeing a shepherd in the fields Moran leaves his son on the road
and hobbles over to ask the way to the town, Bally. The shepherd
points silently with his pipe, and looking in that direction Moran
discerns a faint glow on the horizon. But then he feels that the
shepherd is turning towards him; and his next sentences are an
inexplicable *non sequitur*. 'And I knew I was all alone gazing at that
distant glow . . . spellbound . . . and I was wondering how to
depart without self-loathing or sadness, when a kind of immense
sigh all around me announced it was not I who was departing
but the flock.' He then goes on to describe, in the style of a pas-
toral idyll, the flock returning home, led by the silent shepherd
and followed by his dog.

There is a gap here between the moment when he sensed the
shepherd turning towards him and his knowledge that he was all
alone; and also a contradiction, since the shepherd is ostensibly
still there. Nor is there any apparent reason for self-loathing and

sadness on departing. We remember, however, what happened to
that stranger who stretched out his hand to clutch Moran; and the
single word 'spellbound' here seems significant. It is easy to guess
that another manic fit has occurred in which he has killed the
shepherd. Once again the Moran personality suffers a temporary
blackout while the Molloy one commits the assault so that the
former does not know quite what has happened.

That same night Moran quarrels violently with his son and the
boy runs away with the bicycle and most of the money. It is a
sign of the change that has taken place in his personality that
Moran does not mind much about the money for 'I could no
longer be bothered with these wretched trifles which had once
been my delight.' But the loss of the bicycle is a blow, for he can
hardly walk, and moreover he had intended to learn to pedal
with one foot so as to be independent of the boy.

Now deserted and hardly able to move he remains for days in
an apathetic state, growing ever weaker and looking forward to
losing consciousness. Then suddenly one Sunday he sees Gaber
sitting on a tree stump. Gaber gives him Youdi's instruction to
return home immediately. He will not listen to Moran's protests
that he is sick, abandoned by his son, unable to move and can
bear no more. Gaber merely repeats the message, says that he is
very thirsty and asks for beer. At the end of their conversation
we have yet another *non sequitur* indicating another brain-storm.
'I opened my eyes. I was alone. My hands were full of grass and
earth I had torn up unwittingly and was still tearing up.' Gaber
had vanished as mysteriously as he had arrived, for he was an
hallucination; but his new message indicates the return of the old
Moran personality to something like the state that obtained on the
Sunday of Gaber's first visit, for it calls a halt to the quest for
Molloy.

Moran now begins the long and painful journey back, beset
with 'fiends in human shape and the phantoms of the dead.' His
mind plays with various fantastic theological questions, with the
meaning of the hums and dances of his beloved bees, and with the
four alternative ways of wearing his shirt. It is a nightmare
journey, during which he hears voices giving him orders and
advice, and it lasts throughout autumn and winter. Finally, nearly
dead from starvation and exposure, he arrives home in April to a
deserted house and garden.

His first thoughts are for his flowers and the bees, now dead of
course. Putting his hand in the empty hive he finds a dry light

D

21####### 

ball. 'They had clustered together for a little warmth, to try and sleep. I took out a handful. It was too dark to see. I put it in my pocket. It weighed nothing.' And the next day he looks again at his handful of dead bees, all that was left of the only thing for which he had felt real affection.

Earlier in the story, in his capacity of narrator, Moran had mentioned that he was writing in obedience to an inner voice which he followed more or less in spite of its ambiguity and his hatred for his master. He now tells us that Gaber demands the report that Youdi requires, and also that there is an inner voice, whose words he is at last beginning to understand, which tells him to write. So after spending May and June in the garden in a state of semi-apathy he retires into the house and commences writing his story. Before doing so he has told us that he now has crutches, that he is tired of being a man, and that he intends to clear out and perhaps will at last meet Molloy.

In this Part Two of the first novel. *Molloy*, Beckett has delineated a considerable portion of the whole schizophrenic picture, starting with the precariously integrated and impoverished ego about to break down, continuing through the subjective experience of acute mania and ending with a phase of depression and apathy, partial convalescence, and greatly diminished personality. But this is not the only time Moran has suffered in this way; there have been previous psychotic break-downs when Youdi has sent him on other errands, and he says he could tell us about 'Murphy, Watt, Yerk, Mercier and all the others.' These previous attacks, however, must have been shorter and milder, for they did not lead to such physical disintegration as did his fugue in quest of Molloy. We may expect that soon Youdi (his too powerful super-ego) will make him set out again, this time on crutches, and that his story will be Molloy's.

We are now ready to read Part One, which is concerned with Molloy, the new persona which is formed from Moran's disintegrated mind. That Beckett tells his story first (just as Watt's story was told out of its actual time order) is due to the fact that the id has no knowledge of time. As Freud pointed out, time is the mode in which the ego perceives the outer world; it has meaning only for the ego, not for the id. A disintegrating ego cannot have a consistent appreciation of time, and that is why the accounts which Moran and Molloy give of their journeys leave us guessing as to whether days, months or years elapse.

The story begins with Molloy, now a senile old man lying in bed in what he believes to be his mother's room, waiting for death, and writing disjointed reminiscences and comments on the long journey which led to his collapse on the edge of a forest, from which he was rescued and taken to what is evidently some kind of home for the aged or the mentally deranged. He believes he is in his mother's bed, in her room, but he does not know whether she is dead or not, nor whether he ever had a son, though he sometimes feels he did.

As a matter of fact the first two pages provide us with hints that justify our reading Part Two before Part One. We are told that a man who is always thirsty visits Molloy every Sunday and collects the pages he has written. This man told him that he had started all wrong by actually beginning his story at the beginning! However, this early part was being kept, but Molloy has to start afresh nearer the end of the story; and this is what he is about to do.

Now if we have read Part Two we can easily recognize this man as Gaber again, for we found that Gaber arrived both times on a Sunday, and both times his thirst was mentioned, although it seemed quite irrelevant; moreover, at the end of Moran's story Gaber asks him for his report. And it is equally clear that the 'beginning' which Molloy shouldn't have started with, and which was being kept by 'them', is in fact the report which Moran wrote on his return home and which we have just read in Part Two.

Now we have to deal with Molloy's account which starts at 'nearly the end'. The narrative begins quietly with a somewhat confused recollection of being out in the country one evening, watching two men, A and C, meet on a road. One of them goes on to the town, but the other, who has a stick (later referred to as a club), continues walking uncertainly in the countryside. From his disjointed bits of description and comments one might conclude that these two are projections of different portions of Molloy's ego. Anyhow, this leads immediately to his decision next morning to go and see his mother, of whom he is reminded by hearing the angelus, 'recalling the incarnation'.

This brings us to the central fact about Molloy (who, incidentally, was an only son)—his relationship with his mother. It is one of utter dependency, in one part of himself, masked by disgust and hatred in another part—the hatred being based ostensibly on the fact that she had brought him into the world and 'spoiled the only endurable, just endurable, period of my enormous history.'

His mother, we gather, is an old, mad, blind and deaf woman

living in a town whose name he can never remember. He calls his
mother Mag, and analyses the reason for this very lucidly, revealing the conflict in his mind thereby.

'I called her Mag because for me, without my knowing why, the
letter "g" abolished the syllable "Ma" and as it were spat on it
better than any other letter would have done. And at the same time
I satisfied a deep and doubtless unacknowledged need, the need to
have a Ma, that is a mother and to proclaim it audibly.'

He tells us that he communicated with this wreck of an old
woman by a code of knocks on her skull, reminiscent of the spirit-
raps at a séance. His description of her is as revolting as Swift's of
the Yahoos, but in spite of his hatred he is driven, by his inner
voice, to set forth to find her.

He starts the journey on his bicycle, describing how he manages
with the crutches tied to the cross-bar and his bad leg stretched
out with the foot on the front axle; thus he pedals with one leg,
just as Moran had planned to do. Sometimes he has to walk on the
crutches, pushing his bicycle, or to rest sitting astride it with his
arms on the handle-bars and his head on his arms. It is significant
that his journey started in the second or third week of June, just
as both Moran's journeys started in the summer, for it happens
that early summer is the time of maximum suicides and psychoses.
Professor Kenner, in his excellent *Samuel Beckett*, has treated at
length the symbolism of the bicycle in the novels and plays, connecting it ingeniously with the Cartesian view of the relationship
between body and mind. There is however, another interpretation
possible, psychological rather than metaphysical, and, I feel, quite
as valid here. In modern times the machine, especially when out
of control, appears in dream and phantasy as a symbol of the
passions of the id, replacing the old symbol of wild horses, the
nightmare. Moran, in his relatively normal period, had an autocycle as well as a bicycle, which he left behind. His passions were
under control at that stage. But on his journey, when the id breaks
through the barriers, he is carried on a bicycle which his son rides.
In similar circumstances Molloy rides somewhat uneasily on his
own bicycle, which he eventually abandons. And when they have
lost their bicycles both Moran and Molloy decline rapidly in
strength and physique, and become less passionate, more apathetic,
more eager for death to release them. Incidentally we may note
that Murphy and Watt are passionless, neither have they bicycles.

To return to the story, in which confused memories of the past
are mingled with phantasies and intellectual speculations and

pessimistic comments in such a way that the thread is very easily lost, and only after several readings may the relevance of certain details or comments be appreciated.

Molloy reaches a town, dismounts and rests on the bicycle in the street, is taken to the police station as a vagabond with no papers, but is released, when, for the first time in the story, he remembers his own name. He then rides out of the town, having forgotten why he ever went there, spends the night in a ditch and rides next day into a town which may be the same one again or another one. Here he rides over a dog and falls off his bicycle, is menaced by a hostile crowd but protected by the dog's owner, Mrs Lousse. She takes him to her house where she feeds him and puts him to bed. When he wakes up he finds that he has been washed and shaved, his beard is gone and he is wearing a flimsy nightshirt; moreover the door of the room is locked and the window has bars, and on a chair there is a chamber-pot and a roll of toilet paper. When he shouts for his clothes a 'valet' first tells him they have been burnt, but later on brings them, evidently back from the cleaners. Now all this sounds much more like an asylum than a private house, especially when we learn that the large garden is surrounded by a high wall topped with broken glass.

Molloy spends most of his time in this garden 'drowned in a deep and merciful torpor shot with brief abominable gleams'— i.e. in a state of catatonic stupor. He has paranoid delusions that Lousse spies on him and is trying to poison him by putting depressants and stimulants in his food and drink. The impression of an asylum is strengthened by his remarks that Lousse was flat-chested, had a hairy face and a deep voice, and might indeed have been a man.

Thoughts of Lousse lead him to a memory of a revolting sexual affair with an old woman named Ruth. The significance of this lies in the fact that when he thinks of Lousse and of Ruth, 'God forgive me, to tell you the horrible truth, my mother's image sometimes mingles with theirs, which is literally unendurable.'

The severe conflict between the deeply-repressed incest-wish and the barrier of hatred which the ego has built as a defence against it are clearly to be seen here, and this conflict is at the root of his mental disintegration. It is the cause of his utter disgust with life, of his withdrawal from reality, and also the cause of his need to return to his mother, which he rationalizes as a need 'to settle the matter between us,' though what the matter is he does not explain. 'Yes, so far as I was capable of being bent on any-thing all a lifetime long, and what a lifetime, I had been bent on settling this matter between my mother and me, but had never succeeded.' We may note that the meticulous, calm, 'contrived' Moran (these are his own adjectives) never mentions his mother though he does say that 'Mother Molloy was not completely foreign to me either, it seemed. But she was much less alive than her son . . .' For Moran's is a deeply inhibited personality which has succeeded in burying completely the mother-complex which only achieves expression through the Molloy personality.

One evening, urged by an inner voice which told him to take his crutches and get out, Molloy leaves Mrs Lousse's garden, and wanders into an alley where he attempts suicide by cutting his wrists, but the pain stops him. Before leaving, however, he has pocketed a few silver spoons and one curious object which fasci-nates him because he cannot fathom its purpose; it appeals by its apparent irrationality, as a mystery which he can never hope to solve. It seems like a miniature silver sawing-horse, consisting of four V's, and is of course a knife-rest. It's significance to us lies in the fact that when Moran sat down to dinner waiting to be served he usually played with the knife-rest; and again in the next book of the *Trilogy* the only object saved from Macmann's pockets is a little silver knife-rest. With such easily missed details does Beckett drop clues pointing to the identity of his various charac-ters with one another.

After his abortive suicide Molloy sets out again into the country-side, wandering perhaps months, perhaps years. At some point he comes to the seashore, where he lays in a stock of sixteen pebbles to suck. He spends some time over the problem of how to carry them in his pockets and be sure of taking them each in turn with-out sucking the same one again out of its turn; having solved it for one complete cycle he decides it is just as good to throw fifteen away, keeping only one to suck, and that one 'of course I soon lost, or threw away, or gave away, or swallowed.'

At the seaside his relatively good leg begins to stiffen like the other, which has also shortened, and soon both legs are equally bad though unfortunately not yet of equal length. His physical deterioration increases, he chokes with asthma; at some point his toes drop off, but he stumbles on his journey, through a forest where his progress becomes 'a veritable calvary, with no limit to its stations and no hope of crucifixion.' At intervals in this forest he hears a gong striking.

His wanderings in the forest seem to last throughout a winter and spring; he feeds on mushrooms, roots and berries, and advances only about forty paces a day. At one point he meets a charcoal-burner whom he asks for the way out of the forest, but without getting an intelligible reply. When the man holds him back by the sleeve Molloy suddenly knocks him out with one blow from his crutch, and then deliberately and savagely kicks his body, swinging on both crutches to do so, leaving him perhaps dead perhaps not. The parallel with Moran's attacks on the man whose hand seemed to clutch at him is obvious, though Molloy's account is clearly remembered in detail, while Moran's was not, because the Moran personality was then in abeyance.

When he stumbles onward he tries to avoid the error of going in circles while trying to go in a straight line by the expedient of trying to go in a circle in the hope of thereby achieving a straight line. He reflects that he might have been content to stay in the forest but for the fact that he would feel it was a sin to go against the voices, which he now calls his 'imperatives'.

And this imperative, telling him to get out of the forest, differs only in one point from the former ones, namely in that 'after the usual blarney there followed this solemn warning, perhaps it is already too late.' And he reflects that even if his voice had not faltered and deserted him he still might never have resolved this matter of his mother, for the external world hindered him, and also there was another 'unspoken entreaty' asking him not to do it. 'And of myself, all my life, I think I had been going to my mother, with the purpose of establishing our relations on a less precarious footing. And when I was with her, and I often succeeded, I left without having done anything.'

There is a great sadness in this passage, as over the whole of the final pages where the exhausted cripple crawls on his stomach, using his crutches like grapnels to pull himself forward, covering but fifteen paces a day.

'And I even crawled on my back, plunging my crutches blindly behind me into the thickets and with the black boughs for sky to my closing eyes. I was on my way to my mother. And from time to time I said, Mother, to encourage me I suppose.'

Finally he emerges into the light, and collapses in a ditch on the edge of the forest from where he sees, across a plain, a town which might possibly be his home; but he despairs of being able to drag or roll himself that far. He recalls two apparently insignificant memories, of the two men whom he watched on the road, and of sheep. Both these episodes were purely incidental in Molloy's narrative, but were paralleled in Moran's story where they were highly important. The first man, A, clearly resembled both Moran and the stranger whom Moran killed. The other man, C, is very like Molloy himself and also the other stranger to whom Moran gave bread. In fact A and C, and the two strangers are hallucinatory 'doubles' of the Moran and Molloy personae.

As to the sheep, in Molloy's story the episode merely involved him in wondering whether they were being taken to pasture or to the slaughter-house; and the shepherd did not answer his question but walked silently on; it was a non-event. Moran's story of the encounter with the flock, however, plainly leads one to realize that he murdered the shepherd.

Lying thus in a ditch at the edge of the forest, anticipating death, Molloy hears a voice telling him that help is coming. We are left to infer that he is rescued and taken to the house and bed which he believes to be his mother's and in which he lies writing the story of his 'fugue'.

When Neary affirmed that all life was figure and ground, thus confining it to the external world of sensory perception, Murphy made the significant addition: 'But a wandering to find home.' This admits the whole emotional inner world which can lead to the mystical quest for union with God, or to Schopenhauer's denial of the will-to-live, or to psychopathic phantasies of a return to the womb; and all three hover over the persons of the *Trilogy*. In particular, Molloy's lifelong quest of the mother whom he had hated and rejected is strongly tinged with the womb-phantasy and symbols of this recur throughout the novels: Murphy tied to his rocking-chair, or stewing in his garret; Watt's padded cell; Moran in his warm bed; the small rooms in which both Molloy and Malone lie dying; and finally the jar which encloses Mahood in the last novel of the *Trilogy*.

Although the book is painful and even repellent in many passages, it is nevertheless full of profound insight and compassion, and the closing pages are deeply poetic. The anguish of *King Lear* is mitigated by the remoteness in time of his circumstances from ours, and the horror of the Yahoos by their allegorical nature, but the impact of Molloy on our feelings is immediate, for he is any decrepit tramp we may meet on the road, and any octogenarian decaying into senility in the nearest mental home.

# *Four*

# 'His Rattle Will Make Amends'

THE OLD MAN, now called Malone, lies dying in what he insists is a private room in a private house, not a hospital or asylum, and feeling the end to be very near he plans to tell himself a few stories, enumerate his few remaining possessions, and then 'to die tepidly, without enthusiasm.'

He is quite lucid, though his memory is fitful and he does not know what led up to his present position. He assumes that he must have lost consciousness somewhere, possibly having been hit on the head in a forest which he vaguely remembers, and then brought by an ambulance to this house. At a later stage in his story he considers the possibility that he might be dead already and adds: 'Perhaps I expired in the forest or even earlier.' Clearly he is Molloy at a stage later than that of the previous novel.

Like Molloy, too, he is a misanthrope and has a black view of life, worthy of Timon of Athens.

'Let me say before I go any further that I forgive nobody. I wish them all an atrocious life and then the fires and ice of hell and in the execrable generations to come an honoured name.'

He describes his room and how at first he was tended by an old woman, but now only a hand is put through the door to deposit or take away his soup on the table. He has a stick with a hook so that he can draw the table on its castors towards him or push it away, and can also reach his possessions which are heaped in a corner. And he writes in an exercise book what are ostensibly stories he invents, but actually are his confused memories of past states, intermingled with reflections on his present condition.

His first story is about a boy called Sapo, who reminds one very much of Moran's son. He is described as precocious, unteachable at school although fond of sums so long as they deal with concrete things. He is idle, and given to states of apathetic inertia in which he stands still gazing straight before him, expressionless. Later we learn that 'when he halted it was not the better to think, or the closer to pore upon his dream, but simply because the voice had ceased which told him to go on.'

To supplement these indications of incipient schizophrenia we are also told that he walked with 'stumbling wavering feet' and 'his movements were rather those of one floundering in a quag.'

Sapo likes to wander over the countryside and he visits the peasants, evidently spending some time at the farm of the Lamberts, a family who are described at some length, though they do not seem to have any definite bearing on Malone's life. That Sapo is the boy Malone emerges from various indirections. Thus at one point he breaks off the story to exclaim: 'What tedium. And I call that playing. I wonder if I am not talking yet again about myself. Shall I be incapable, to the end, of lying on any other subject?' A few pages later he interrupts himself to say irrelevantly: 'We are getting on. Nothing is less like me than this patient reasonable child, struggling all alone for years to shed a little light upon himself.'

On the next page he wakes after a short sleep and, feeling an unwelcome return to his former frenzy against the living, he calms himself, and we read: 'I stop everything and wait. Sapo stands on one leg, motionless, his strange eyes closed.'

In the paragraph which follows he is talking throughout in the first person, but the content of the first half of it, concerning his inability as a child to play with others and his being beaten by grown-ups and hounded back into the games, all seems to apply naturally to Sapo, who had just been referred to. And there are other passages where there is an ambiguous confusion between the first and third persons.

At the end of the Lamberts episode Sapo tells the daughter that he is going away and will not return. The narrative is immediately broken off while Malone indulges in various reflections. He recalls his searchings for solutions to the mystery of life, first of all with psychoanalysts. 'One day I took counsel of an Israelite on the subject of conation,' i.e. he studied Freud's libido theory; then he turned to oriental mysticism, 'I then tried, for a space, to lay hold of a kindred spirit among the inferior races, red, yellow, chocolate, and so on;' and nearly succeeded with the insane, 'with the insane too I failed, by a hair's breadth.' But this topic is not pursued, for he continues with considerations about his present circumstances. Unfortunately he drops his pencil and two days elapse unrecorded, before he can resume writing. Yet they have brought him 'the solution and conclusion of the whole sorry business, I mean the business of Malone (since that is what I am called now) and of the other, for the rest is no business of mine. And it was, though more unutterable, like the crumbling away of two little heaps of finest sand, or dust, or ashes, of unequal size, but diminishing together as it were in ratio, if that means anything, and leaving behind them, each in its own stead, the blessedness of absence.'

The exact nature of 'the other' is not elucidated; it could be Sapo, or it could be all the repressed part of Malone's personality (the Jungian Shadow) or it could be the essential Self; but the experience is one of dissolution into nothingness; and yet simultaneously with this experience Malone was searching for his pencil and observing his surroundings, and even observing also the dissolution of his two selves! For the essentially irrational experience can be spoken of only in contradictory and illogical terms.

After this digression he 'finds' Sapo again, but now he is different; he is sitting on a bench apparently in the harbour of a small town, dressed in a very long, old, green great-coat and wearing an old, dirty hard hat, seemingly a bowler. He is, in fact, remarkably like Watt and Molloy, and Malone discards the name Sapo and adopts the name Macmann for this transformed person, who sits there oblivious of the time of day or season of the year, in a state of apathy. However, this immobility is not permanent, for we are told that he will wander for years and that all his old age is in front of him. In fact we soon see him lying prostrate on the ground, in pouring rain, clutching the tufts of grass, on some open plain, looking, with his long dirty-white hair, very like Molloy, and, like him too, thinking that this life is a punishment for the sin of having been born. He evidently is no longer young, for Malone comments that he must be strong 'to have reached the age he has just reached and which is nothing or very little compared to the age he will reach, as I know to my cost, without any serious mishap.' The parenthesis is a clear indication of his identity with Malone, just as is a previous sentence referring to Malone's approaching death: 'Then it will be all over with the Murphys, Merciers, Molloys, Morans, and Malones, unless it goes on beyond the grave.'

Macmann was unemployable, for when put to weeding he would dig up the flowers or vegetables, and when working as a scavenger he left the street worse than he found it, having collected all the miscellaneous rubbish and muck and put it carefully on the pavement or in the middle of the road.

After enduring the rain for a time Macmann starts to roll himself in the arc of a huge circle over the plain. This plain, or a
waste land, or empty seashore—they symbolize the limbo in
which the schizophrenic lives during the phase of almost total
withdrawal from the outer world. Moran, Molloy, Macmann
wander over a featureless plain; an empty seashore appears in
*Molloy*, *Embers* and outside Hamm's house in *Endgame*; in *Happy
Days* Winnie sits in an endless empty plain; in *Godot* the landscape
is empty save for one tree; empty space surrounds the characters
in *Play*; and *How It Is* is set in an infinite expanse of mud.

Another recurrent feature in the works is the concern with
small objects of no intrinsic worth, whose role seems to be to
attach the ego to this world, or to act as lifebuoys to which the
unstable self clings to save him from drowning in the sea of non-
existence. The impulse to collect small useless objects, stones, or
scraps of metal or what not, has been observed with many schizo-
phrenics—for instance Hölderlin and Dr Navratil's patient,
Alexander.*

Malone tells over his possessions lovingly, for he has positive
affection for little portable things. 'I loved to finger and caress the
hard shapely objects that were there in my deep pockets, it was
my way of talking to them and reassuring them.' And he makes it
clear that, being immature in his emotions, this feeling for objects,
such as a stone, a horse-chestnut, or a fircone, was a satisfactory
substitute for personal contacts and for religion.

The actual objects that he enumerates include some which have
significance elsewhere, with others that do not. Amongst them
are a single boot, originally yellow (Watt wore a single brown
boot), a brimless old hat like a bell-glass (cf. Watt's and Macmann's hats), a blood-stained club (cf. Molloy), a stone (again
Molloy), the cap of a bicycle bell (Molloy cherished the little horn
of his bicycle), the top half of a crutch (Moran and Molloy had
crutches), and some buttons (both Watt's and Macmann's overcoat buttons were specially noted earlier). All these are obviously
significant correspondences. Other objects might have some
relevance, but if so it is not obvious. Malone has kept the bowl of
a broken pipe; he is not a smoker, and the only previous personage
who smoked a pipe was the shepherd to whom Moran spoke in
Ballyba. In answer to his query as to where the town lay, the
shepherd pointed with his pipe; the account is rather equivocal,
but it leads one to infer that in a manic moment he killed the

* See L. Navratil, *Schizophrenie und Sprache*.

shepherd, and that his sudden knowledge that he was all alone, and his unease at this, represent an awakening from the attack, while his subsequent description of the flock departing, the shepherd silent in front of them, is a phantasy to absolve himself. That he should pocket the broken pipe-bowl is entirely typical.

Another enigmatic possession is a packet, light as a feather, containing something soft wrapped up in newspaper which is yellow with age. Malone regards it lovingly but cannot recall what it reminds him of, nor does he undo it to see, but puts it away to keep as a mystery. He wonders if it is a lac of rupees or a lock of hair; but surely it can only be that little dry ball which was all that remained of Moran's beloved bees when he returned. 'They had clustered together for a little warmth, to try to sleep. I took out a handful. It was too dark to see. I put it in my pocket. It weighed nothing.' I am sure that Moran treasured this cluster of dead bees, wrapped it up in newspaper, and carried it in his pocket as a memento of one of the very few things in this world which had aroused his affection. And Malone knew it was something he had once loved, in one of his former states, though he could not remember exactly what it was. But of course this interpretation is purely my personal one, based not upon positive clues but on my feeling that practically everything in these novels has a definite purpose and carries a significant connotation.

Having gone through the inventory of his possessions Malone resumes the tale of Macmann, whom he had left rolling over a plain. We are simply told that he regains consciousness much later in an asylum, the House of Saint John of God (which was casually mentioned by Wylie in *Murphy*). There is obviously a gap between the time when he was on the plain and that when he wakes in the asylum, but we are never told what experiences he went through during the interval, anymore than in the analogous cases of Watt after he left the railway station, or Molloy after he fell in the ditch at the edge of the forest, or Malone in the period immediately before he found himself in this room where he is dying.

Macmann is now evidently an old man, but not a dying one. He clamours for his clothes and his things, particularly his hat, but all the small things in his pockets had been thrown away with the notable exception of a little silver knife-rest, that important link between him, Moran and Molloy. He is tended by an old woman called Moll during the initial period of his stay; just as Malone at first was looked after by a woman, though after a while only a hand was poked through the doorway to give him his meals. Moll it is who recovers Macmann's battered old hat and 'contemplated with tenderness the old bewildered face relaxing, and in its tod of hair the mouth trying to smile, and the little red eyes* turning timidly towards her as if in gratitude or rolling towards the recovered hat, and the hands raised to set it more firmly and returning to rest trembling on the blanket.'

This pathetic picture of helpless old age is followed by a nauseating account of their futile attempts to make love, with Moll writing him gushing little notes, and regretting that they had not met sixty years ago. It is evidently a variant of the Molloy-Ruth episode, treated with the sentimentality appropriate to second-childishness. But this ridiculous situation does not last very long, for Moll decays and dies.

With her death the second phase of Macmann's life in the asylum begins, and a curious figure called Lemuel takes over the duty of attending to him. Lemuel is both an assistant in the asylum who looks after patients and also himself evidently insane, for sometimes he would stand rooted to the spot in a daze, while at other times he would stamp about, shouting unintelligibly and hitting himself with a hammer on the shins or on the head. At Macmann's urgent entreaty Lemuel allows him to get up and wander in the garden, so by now he is evidently recovering some of his strength. He used to go out in all weathers, and hide from the keepers when they called him in. But Lemuel would find him hidden in a bush, and he would creep in too and they would sit huddled together, bound by the same mutual attraction that linked Murphy with Mr Endon, and Watt with Sam. However, Lemuel also punished Macmann for tearing off a branch or for grubbing up a hyacinth, and Macmann was not contented with his situation but tried to find some breach in the walls of the grounds through which to escape, though in vain.

At this point let us consider Malone again. There have been various disjointed remarks inserted in his narration which indicate a progressively febrile condition. When telling of the loss of his pencil, for instance, he suddenly says: 'But why this sudden heat, has anything happened, anything changed?' Then, in the middle of his account of Moll we read: 'I pause to record that I feel in extraordinary form. Delirium perhaps.' A couple of pages later he says there are a thousand little things he could mention but he has

---

* We may remember that Moran had 'little ferrety eyes'—i.e. they were pink.

realized that when he writes things down his notes seem to negate themselves. 'So I hasten to turn aside from this extraordinary heat, to mention only it, which has seizèd on certain parts of my economy, I will not specify which. And to think I was expecting rather to grow cold, if anything.'

Thus we may understand as a product of delirium the account he gives of an attack on him made by a mysterious visitor. This is interpolated between the mention of Macmann's request to be allowed up and the description of him walking in the grounds. Malone felt a sudden violent blow on his head, and there was a strange man standing by his bed. He describes how although the man spoke he heard nothing. Apparently the visitor came in the morning, left for lunch, then returned in the afternoon, spending altogether about seven hours in the room. He was well but sombrely dressed. 'I took him at first for the undertaker's man, annoyed at having called prematurely.' He kept on looking at his watch, he had a tightly rolled umbrella, and though his suit was black he wore brown boots that were caked with mud. His silence, his neat dress but muddy boots, and the emphasis placed on the watch and umbrella suggest that the visitor is really an hallucinatory projection of the repressed Moran personality which persisted in Malone's unconscious. Malone tried to ask him to pick up the stick which he had dropped, but his own voice had gone, so he planned to write down a list of questions in case the visitor should return next day, but this does not happen. After some rather wandering reflections Malone continues:

'What light! Foretaste of paradise? My head. On fire, full of burning oil. . . . The pain is almost unbearable, upon my soul it is. Incandescent migraine.'

It is not surprising that the final pages of his story of Macmann should have the quality of a delirious phantasy and be cut short by the narrator's death. All that he has told us of Macmann up to now has had the quality of reminiscence, even if the memories are distorted or confused, like the stories of Moran and Molloy. But the account of the expedition organized by Lady Pedal to give the inmates of John of God's a treat, plausibly though it begins, soon becomes the product of mania.

Lemuel is to be in charge of the party of five inmates who are privileged to go on this excursion to the islands, and he collects their rations of soup in a bucket, from which he extracts the six pieces of bacon, eats all the fat and throws the rinds back into the soup. Then he visits the five cells to dish out the soup.

The first cell contains a young man seated in a rocking-chair seemingly asleep, except that his eyes are open; he stays inert unless made to move, and he corresponds closely to Murphy.

The second inmate, called the Saxon, who is tall and stiff, and who apparently goes outside occasionally but soon hastens back after glimpsing the outside world, has the 'air of perpetually looking for something while at the same time wondering what that something could possibly be.' He has an obvious affinity with Watt, and it is hardly unintentional that we read 'What! he exclaimed' inserted without any apparent relevance in the account being given of him.

The third cell contains a small thin active man with white hair, who has a cloak folded over his arm and an umbrella. He could be Moran, whose umbrella was an important item in his story. And the fourth cell holds a big bearded misshapen man sprawling on the floor, occupied in scratching himself: he is referred to as 'the giant' and reminds one of Molloy, whom Moran described as being 'massive and hulking, to the point of misshapenness.'

These four, together with Macmann, are the group which Lemuel gathers to wait the arrival of Lady Pedal and the waggonette. The youth and the thin man are tied together at the ankles and so are the Saxon and the giant, while Macmann is firmly gripped by Lemuel. When Lady Pedal appears they all get into the waggonette, together with two sailors, and drive down towards the sea. In her effort to make the party go Lady Pedal bursts into song, but it is not a success. The youth is talking to himself, asking and answering questions. His dialogue repeats scraps of the song that Watt heard sung by a distant choir: 'And you? . . . Thanks. . . . and you? . . . Thanks.'

On reaching the shore they embark in a boat and are rowed over to the islands by the two sailors; Lady Pedal, trailing her hand in the water, laments that only she can appreciate the beauty of the scene. And Malone interjects: 'My creatures, what of them? Nothing. They are there, each as best he can, as best he can be somewhere.' The initial phrase reminds us of the 'my people' that Beckett uses to refer to his whole range of vagabonds.

During this narrative Malone's condition has deteriorated and his end is near.

'And I? Indubitably going, that's all that matters. . . . Grandiose suffering. I am swelling. What if I should burst? The ceiling rises and falls, rises and falls, rhythmically, as when I was a foetus. Also to be mentioned a noise of rushing water. . . .' He feels that he is being born into death, feet first, and that his head will be the last bit to die.

On arriving at the island Lady Pedal goes off with one of the sailors to find a spot to picnic on; the thin one and the boy disembark and the boy throws himself down in the shade of a rock (remember how Murphy envied Belacqua) thus preventing the thin one from running about as he wanted. The giant will not leave the boat, so the Saxon can't do so either. And now the delirium sets in. Lemuel kills the remaining sailor with his hatchet, at which the Saxon applauds and the thin one breaks his umbrella (symbol of Moran's remnant of normal sanity?). The first sailor returns and Lemuel kills him also, and when Lady Pedal comes back and faints at the sight of the two murdered sailors the Saxon screams for her to be killed too. It is not made clear whether Lemuel murders her or merely leaves her stranded, but only he and the five patients get into the boat to float away.

Malone is at his last gasp and we read: 'Gurgles of outflow', a phrase that harks back to a much earlier remark when he felt that 'In my head I suppose all was streaming and emptying away as through a sluice,' as well as to his recent mention of the noise of rushing water.

In the final paragraphs he sees the tangle of grey bodies, which is 'my creatures' in the boat, and an array of lights from the sky, sea and the hills. He sees Lemuel raise the hatchet, but knows he will never hit anyone again, and in broken phrases, in which he confuses himself and his possessions with Lemuel and the hatchet, he murmurs: '. . . he will not touch anyone any more, either with it, . . . or with his hammer, or with his stick or with his fist . . . or with his pencil . . .' until the detached phrases trail off to nothing.

It seems curious to me that previous commentators, while showing such insight into so many of the philosophical meanings of the novels, and half apprehending the identity of all the protagonists, should have failed to see that the schizophrenic nature of the hero, to which so many obvious clues have been given, resolves their difficulties. The authors of *The Testament of Samuel Beckett* take the view that all the protagonists, of the plays as well as the novels, are aspects of Man in general, a universal man whom they call Q, short for Quidam. Murphy, Molloy, Hamm, Krapp, etc., are separate individual embodiments of Q. 'This omnipresent figure should be referred to as Malone, Molloy, Estragon, Watt, etc., only in specific contexts. In its omnipresent whole it

E

contains their composite identities.' Now in my view the *Trilogy* presents one man whose various schizophrenic phases are described under the names of Sapo, Moran, Macmann, Molloy and Malone, with the Unnamable and Pim as his post-mortem states. But the various characters of the plays, Krapp, Mrs Rooney, Winnie, are all separate individuals, and the couples Estragon-Vladimir, Hamm-Clov are different split personalities.

Mr Fletcher, in his excellent study of *The Novels Of Samuel Beckett*, though he treats the protagonists as separate individuals, fleetingly comes near the truth. While missing all the pointers to the schizophrenic change of Moran into Molloy and never realizing that Moran's story comes first, nevertheless he does say that Moran only finds Molloy 'in the sense that and in so far as he becomes Molloy.' And he refers to Malone as a reincarnation of Molloy and Murphy, but evidently means only that he is another attempt by Beckett to portray a man searching for his real self.

Mr Fletcher accepts Moran as being a sort of detective employed by a real agency (Messrs Gaber and Youdi) to find another individual called Molloy.

R. N. Coe, on the other hand, takes Moran to be an 'allegorical figure' representing a rational integer, in contrast to Molloy who is the 'irrational number', and considers the former a contrived character who does not achieve the rich humanity of Molloy. Neither Coe nor Fletcher realizes that Moran is the central person in the *Trilogy* and that Beckett has delineated him in his near-normal state in far more detail than he has depicted any of the others. He has given us numerous details of Moran's appearance, dress, habits, relationship with others (his son, his cook, his priest, his neighbours), so that we know far more about the Moran who existed before his 'fugue' transformed him into Molloy than we do about his psychotic personalities—which is only natural since the disintegrated ego has lost so much of its former content.

Beckett has been at pains to give the attentive reader numerous clues showing that he is dealing with a multiple personality: apart from Malone's various possessions there are other significant coincidences. Thus Moran, Molloy and Macmann's hard domed hats have a crack in them; all the tramps are particularly interested in birds—Moran loves the song birds, Molloy remarks on the corncrakes; Sapo is fascinated by the hawk; and both Moran and Sapo are concerned about a grey hen. All these things, ambiguous though each one may be, nevertheless add up to the conclusion that the various names denote different personality groupings of one disintegrated ego.

These different personalities reveal between them almost all the standard clinical symptoms and the different phases of schizophrenia. Malone (to adopt his final name) begins as the schizoidal boy Sapo, whose chief characteristic is his tendency to apathy. We are not told, but we may guess, that he eventually went to college and saw something of London and Europe; later we find him as the middle-aged, self-centred, 'contrived' Moran who has 'turned towards the outer world as towards the lesser evil.' This restricted ego is not stable, for before his final break-down he has had shorter and less damaging attacks in which, as he tells us, Youdi has sent him in search of others such as Watt and Yerk.

Even before the Molloy search begins Moran has shown the characteristic symptoms: disorder of thought, incongruous emotional reactions, paranoid suspicions, deep depression, uncontrolled sudden rages. And when the Molloy personality begins to emerge, i.e. in the acute catatonic phase, there are outbreaks of manic violence, periods of stupor, catatonic movements, inner voices, hallucinations, and gross bodily deterioration.

Molloy's stay in Lousse's house and Macmann's in St. John of God's may easily be two versions of one period in an asylum; the old man who tells the stories can only retrieve confused and disjointed memories of what his different personalities have endured. But they could just as easily relate to two different asylums, since one cannot disentangle objective facts from the maze of phantasy and distorted perception.

It is, of course, quite usual for a schizophrenic to have several different periods in an asylum or mental home separated by longer or shorter periods when his condition has improved sufficiently for him to be discharged. One of Dr Navratil's patients, Alexander, first entered the Gugging Sanatorium at the age of twenty, and after a few months treatment was released. Two years later he had to be treated again and was released after four months. Then three years after this he developed delusions of persecution and auditory hallucinations, but could be released after three months' treatment by electric shock. His improvement this time was only short-lived and he had to be re-admitted as a permanent patient. It is interesting to note that Alexander had a compulsive urge to hurt himself and would beat his face with his fists until it bled; just as Lemuel hit his head and shins with his hammer.

One can easily see that a patient with a history of several periods in different asylums might regard them as belonging to different persons who yet mysteriously seemed intimately connected with himself; and at times also he might recognize their identity with himself. This is precisely the position of Malone.

This reading of the two novels is necessarily somewhat incomplete, for Beckett deliberately leaves many lacunae in the stories and many of his statements are ambiguous; he is presenting an irrational, schizophrenic experience. But I am sure that these novels depict a mixture of phantasies and actual experiences, interwoven inextricably, of the several split-off portions of one mind. Malone's life has been an agony, and we can only hope that, as with Murphy, 'his rattle will make amends.' Knowing Beckett, however, we may well doubt it.

# *Five*

# 'Off, Off, You Lendings'

Wɪᴛʜ *Molloy* and *Malone Dies* Beckett has surely told the tale of the old man, meted want with a span, assessed the sum of the world's woes. What else remains to be said? Only that last, impossible task—'Nothingness in words enclose.' And this is just the theme of the final book of the *Trilogy*, *The Unnamable*, which presents the old man, now free from 'this muddied vesture of decay', in a post-mortem limbo searching for, and also recoiling from, that essential 'I' which may be supposed to underlie his manifest existence. This inner, eternal Self, which, as the Upanishads say, is 'the only one free from qualities,' is thereby describable only in negatives and contradictions, so that it has always been called a Nothingness and yet has always been regarded not as a mere emptiness but as a positive source of being. As such it is both infinite and incommensurable with the concepts of our thought, dependent as these are on space and time. In Murphy's phrase, it is 'a matrix of surds', and incidentally it is worth noting that in this book Murphy is mentioned no less than seven times as being an earlier persona of the protagonist.

The book starts off with three fundamental questions about space, identity and time, followed by a half-hearted attempt to assert the fact of his existence; and these will be developed with ever more complicated ramifications throughout the whole novel.

'Where now? Who now? When now? Unquestioning. I, say I. Unbelieving. Questions, hypotheses, call them that. Keep going, going on, call that going, call that on.'

And the reader asks who is speaking and where is he? It is clear almost immediately that this is the post-mortem existence of Malone and all his personae—but what exactly has survived?

The answer to this question involves us in some discussion about the nature of mind and of personality. To say Malone's mind is what survives is to beg too many questions. Just what is his mind? Does it include the consciousness of Molloy, Moran, etc? Is it merely the complex of factors which constitute Malone's ego as it was at the time of his death? Or is it a sort of mental film on which all his lifetime of mental experiences, his perceptions, his ideas, his impulses, etc., etc., are recorded and preserved? Or just a set of behaviour patterns characteristic of him rather than of anyone else, and thus constituting his personality? On this last view Keyserling has pointed out that 'Precisely those tendencies which seem to be particularly personal, demonstrably do not lead to infinity,' because they only have meaning in this phenomenal world.

In a very interesting paper on *Personal Identity and Survival* (a Myers memorial lecture, published by the Society for Psychical Research ) Professor C. D. Broad elaborated his theory that a Person is a compound of two factors: his body (with all its physical processes) and what Broad calls a psi-component, which is not quite the Cartesian 'mind', but a mental something which carries some of the dispositional basis for the experiences of knowing, willing, and feeling; but we need not hold either that this psi-component by itself is a person or that it is unextended or un-located merely because it is discarnate. He points out that we know of physical existents, such as an electro-magnetic field or the beam transmitting a piece of music during a broadcast, which are not material bodies but yet are extended and located somewhere. Professor Broad then suggests that such a psi-component might persist after death and might have a 'quasi-personal dream-like stream of experience.' And later he elaborates this as follows:

'But it would not be inconceivable that there would be a stream of delusive quasi-perceptual experiences, as of speaking, listening, reading, writing, doing and suffering, such as we have in our dreams. And it is not inconceivable that there might be a core of feeling or of imagery, qualitatively like that which one gets from one's body during one's life-time, but not actually arising from an organism and its internal processes.'

We may consider that *The Unnamable* is an account of such a stream of delusive experiences of the psi-component of the old man after Malone's death. In the main they are experiences 'as of' speaking and remembering, and they illustrate very well the picture of the next world suggested by Professor H. H. Price in a paper entitled 'Survival and the Idea of Another World' (in Part 182 of the *Proceedings of the Society for Psychical Research*). Professor Price suggests that the post-mortem state would be a world of mental images, just as real as the images which occur in dreams, the source of these images being the memories and desires of the person, including those repressed desires of which he was unconscious in his lifetime, but which now, in this private solipsistic world, might stand in no need of repression—a rather disturbing idea, but one which obviously fits in with Professor Broad's concept of the psi-component.

For the first few pages the surviving component of Malone is occupied in trying to locate himself and account intelligibly for what he experiences. The first image that arises is that of Malone, wearing his brimless hat, apparently circling round him, though shortly afterwards he is changed to Molloy. For convenience, to avoid confounding the persons, I will refer to this surviving entity, the psi-component of the multiple personality who died as Malone, as M.

M, then, considers that he is in a probably vast, dark empty space, and he chooses to think that he is fixed at the centre of it—an appropriate assumption for a solipsist. He also thinks that he has been here ever since he began to be: '. . . my appearances elsewhere having been put in by other parties.' And as to these other parties: 'To tell the truth I believe they are all here, at least from Murphy on.'

In the midst of his discussion of the fact that he has heard sounds he drops into a significant complaint: 'If only I were not obliged to manifest.' And a page later on we read: 'Why did I have myself represented in the midst of men, the light of day? It seems to me it was none of my doing. We won't go into that now. I can see them still, my delegates.' But the answer to his question was given by the living Malone: 'The forms are many in which the unchanging seeks relief from its formlessness.' But these forms are 'lendings' which must be cast off if the fundamental 'unaccommodated man' is to be revealed.

It is from these 'delegates', or vice-existers, as he also calls them, that M. has learnt about mankind and life in the world. They formed and educated his 'personality', one called Basil having apparently had an important influence. One of their favourite subjects was mother, and another was God, but their chief emphasis was on his fellow men; they also taught him about love, intelligence, counting and reason. Like Molloy, M. was born in Bally.

M. endeavours, in order to reach his true 'me', to abolish all these 'delegates', Murphy, Molloy, Malone, etc., as well as God, man, nature, saying that he invented them all 'to seek relief from formlessness'.

'I invented love, music, the smell of flowering currant, to escape from me. Organs, a without, it's easy to imagine, a god, it's unavoidable, you imagine them, it's easy, the worst is dulled, you doze away an instant.'

That the external world of perceptions, concepts, and persons is created not as a manifestation and fulfilment of the real Self, but as a means of escape from its own self-awareness, is a special Beckettian compound of Philosophic Idealism with Existentialism.

But M. cannot in fact wholly dispense with phenomena and personality; he is forced to continue conjuring up images and above all pouring out words; he speaks because otherwise he would cease to exist. He even thinks he may be obliged to create another 'delegate' and he calls to mind Basil, whom he now re-christens Mahood, and whose saga he will shortly relate.

First, however, he harks back to a favourite theme, the view that birth is the original sin, which Calderon expressed in the line

'Man's greatest crime is ever to have been born.'

To M. it appears that he has been given a task to perform, but he is quite in the dark as to what the task is, or what is required of him by his master, or perhaps group of masters.

'I was given a pensum, at birth perhaps as a punishment for having been born perhaps, or for no particular reason, because they dislike me, and I've forgotten what it is. But was I ever told?' He willingly concedes that his master probably wishes him well and that the task is for his own good; but why has the master never explained what he wants, nor in what ways M. falls short? It is a Kafkaesque situation, like that of Joseph K. in *The Trial*. He considers various possibilities as to the nature of this task, and the lesson which he supposes he has to say, and what his unknown master may be like, but finally retires to a purely negative position: 'Having nothing to say, no words but the words of others, I have to speak. No-one compels me to, there is no one, it's an accident, a fact.' In fact, his Existence depends on expression through speech: in the beginning of the microcosm, as of the macrocosm, is 'The Word'.

So he starts to talk about yet another 'delegate', Mahood, who affirms what M. denies, namely his identity with M. Yet M. begins relating Mahood's story in the first person, thus assuming this identity.

Mahood, then, starts as a one-legged cripple hobbling in a

curve over a barren landscape, returning to his home and family. He finds himself inside a vast yard, surrounded by high walls, in the midst of which is a windowless rotunda furnished with loop-holes, from which all the members of his family watch his incredibly slow progress. Apparently whole years go by, during which the family exchange interested comments with each other. Finally they all die of ptomaine poisoning before he reaches the rotunda, by which time he has somehow managed to lose an arm. When at last he does enter, it is to stamp maniacally on their decomposing corpses. The whole story is another insane phantasy, one more variant of the journey through the 'Molloy country' that has already been endured by Moran, Molloy and Macmann, as indeed the setting of yard, walls and windowless rotunda, which inevitably remind us of an asylum, hints.

After this there is an interlude in which M. resumes his monologue in his own person, lamenting that all his words and ideas have been learned from these vice-existers, and that he can only speak of the things that do not concern the real 'me', things '. . . that they have crammed me full of to prevent me saying who I am, where I am, and from doing what I have to do in the only way that can put an end to it.' But he persists in the struggle to assert his identity, to utter 'me', and to deny that he was Murphy, Watt, etc., '. . . who told me I was they, who I must have tried to be, under duress, or through fear, or to avoid acknowledging me.' This passage reveals the quintessence of the schizophrenic situation, the inability to achieve a true autonomous identity.

After this, M. relapses into the Mahood persona and relates how, after travelling in loops over the island, sometimes on hands and knees, finally crawling on his belly or rolling over the ground (compare Molloy and Macmann) he ends up as an armless, legless trunk stuck in a deep jar near the shambles in a quiet street. The jar is placed opposite a chophouse, whose proprietress looks after him to the extent of cleaning out the jar once a week, occasionally feeding him a marrow-bone, and covering him with a tarpaulin when it snows. Descriptions of Mahood's life in the jar alternate with attempts by M. to resume his search for his true self, and it is not immediately obvious to the reader when the changes occur, since the pronoun 'I' is used by both parties. In the end Mahood just peters out, as M. merely withdraws himself from Mahood's world (like Moran leaving the 'Molloy' country) and says that the stories of Mahood are ended.

In M's meditations, sandwiched in between parts of Mahood's

story, he considers first how to placate 'the other' (his master) and also the 'delegates' who insist on his existence in them.

'It's a lot to expect of one creature, It's a lot to ask, that he should first behave as if he were not, then as if he were, before being admitted to that peace where he neither is, nor is not, and where the language dies that permits of such expressions.' And again he slips out of this mystical mood, for he feels that the exhortations to be himself, which he hears, come by the same channel as that of the other voices, those of the vice-existers. In an attempt to realize his fundamental Self, 'his glassy essence', he imagines one named Worm. Worm is 'if not me, a step towards me.' He attributes no qualities to Worm, who knows nothing, has no voice or reason, and does not even appreciate the distinction between himself and the rest—i.e. between subject and object. Nevertheless M., as Worm, is subject to the urge to be incarnated, the Schopenhauerian Will which is at the basis of all his 'imperatives', those voices which force him always to 'go on'. He reflects on the experience of life in the world above:

'The common lot. A harmless joke. That will not last for ever. For me to gather while I may. They mentioned roses. I'll smell them before I'm finished. Then they'll put the accent on the thorns. What prodigious variety. The thorns they'll have to come and stick into me, as into their unfortunate Jesus.'

But Worm finds great difficulty in acquiring the senses of hearing and sight, and a body, or of setting himself in motion towards the world of nature. In any case, M. reflects, if Worm were to get these qualities he would thereby cease to be Worm, but would become Mahood. He imagines that 'they', in the light, have made holes in the wall surrounding his dark pit and are calling to Worm, encouraging him to burst through and be born. But if Worm will not move 'they' will perhaps retire, even block up the holes in the wall, and be punished for their failure by the 'master'. After pages of highly confusing speculation he arrives at the idea that perhaps he is really the partition, two surfaces with no thickness, dividing the world from the mind and not belonging to either. On this view the Self would seem to be the interaction of mind and body, and analogous to the surface-tension between, say, water and oil.

But he harks back to the experiences of his life-time, summarizing the essentials of the previous novels: 'I would have liked to lose me, lose me the way I could long ago, when I still had some imagination, close my eyes and be in a wood, or on the seashore, or in a town where I don't know anyone, it's night, everyone has gone home, I walk the streets, I lash into them one after the other, it's the town of my youth, I'm looking for my mother to kill her. . . .'

And this is soon followed by an allegory of the futility of worldly occupations (rather reminiscent of the porter wheeling milkcans in *Watt*) in which he yearns for something active to do, to convince himself of his existence; for example, to have many vessels, half to be emptied of water and the other half to be filled, so that he could go with his thimble and carry the water with the utmost care from the ones to the others. But he reflects that 'they' would arrange to mislead him by connecting the tanks with pipes and taps so as to make the levels the same.

The monologue becomes even more difficult to follow, with its continual shiftings from 'I' to 'he' and 'they', all in phrases separated by commas. M. oscillates continuously between the affirmation and the denial of the Will to Live, and also keeps on harking back to the life which he has known, though the 'I' that experienced it is not the true 'I' that he is seeking. The voice of this true self is what M. is always aware of, but never able to make his own.

After talking for several more pages about his own incapacity to express himself, to understand who or where he is, with references to a door through which he should go to find the silence, he once more confesses that all the stories about paralytic travellers are his stories, or possibly memories, for he doesn't know for certain whether he has lived already, or is living, or will live, but he continues to assert both that he has never stirred from this limbo where he is, and that 'it's not I'.

Then M. changes to an attempt to explain the nature of 'he' whose story should be told but that, being 'the silence', he has no story, nevertheless the attempt must be made: '. . . in the old stories incomprehensibly mine, to find his, it must be there somewhere, it must have been mine before being his, I'll recognize it, in the end I'll recognize it, the story of the silence that he never left, that I should never have left'; and if only M. can find that silence then 'he' and 'I' would be united, the end and the beginning would coincide.

This is pure mysticism, differing from Christian mysticism in that it dispenses with the images of a personal God and a personal Soul, but having obvious affinities with Hindu mysticism and in particular with Schopenhauer's doctrine of Will. It is this Will which creates and maintains the world of phenomena, and which continually incarnates in living beings. But when the individual, say Malone, dies his psi-component (M.) is still actuated by the Will, although also, since on earth he had attained a sufficient degree of intellect and had also suffered sufficiently, he is able to want to deny the Will. So in *The Unnamable* we have this continual oscillation between assertion and denial. But the Will, endeavouring to incarnate and express itself by means of the psi-component, can only achieve an unsubstantial world of images; it can invent stories, which, however, do not have quite the conviction or intensity of life. So M. constantly complains that he only has words, and must utter words, and must tell stories; but he always feels that the words are inadequate, and he is always yearning to deny the Will and achieve the silence which is, paradoxically, not Nothing, but the unmanifest Will, the origin of everything, the 'matrix of Surds'. But this yearning for Nirvana, for the annihilation of self, is not satisfied and the book ends with the Will still in command;

'You must say words, as long as there are any, until they find me, until they say me, . . . perhaps they have said me already, perhaps they have carried me to the threshold of my story, before the door that opens on my story, that would surprise me, if it opens, it will be I, it will be the silence, where I am, I don't know, I'll never know, in the silence you don't know, you must go on, I can't go on, I'll go on.'

Undoubtedly *The Unnamable* is a difficult book to read. After the first fourteen pages paragraphs are abandoned, full stops become rare, and the stream of thought rolls on rather like Molly Bloom's famous monologue, only with the complication that the referents of the pronoun 'I' are continually changing. Throughout the book Beckett is faced with the insoluble problem which all mystics have faced, of how to express in terms of the concepts which we have derived from our phenomenal world something which has been experienced in the noumenal world. Any such experience, when translated into words, can only be expressed in paradoxes, logical contradictions and phrases which are verbally absurd. Poets (and Beckett is pre-eminently a poet) can convey something by means of imagery, but when put into abstract philosophical terms it reduces to such forms as 'A is both A and Not-A,' or 'The whole is contained in the part.'

M. is imprisoned within a circle of man-made concepts, 'I', 'he', 'they', 'the master', 'delegates', 'the silence', and his monologue revolves in circles continuously, unable to escape and reach the ultimate unknown centre. The paths of his 'delegates' on their journeys on earth, circular, in a great arc, or in a spiral are symbols of this inability to go directly to the centre.

The whole *Trilogy* is a very profound work which may be read on several different levels. As narrative, it is a compassionate and moving study of old age, and a bitter, pessimistic comment on human life and its inherent suffering. Even here, however, there are occasional touches which reveal a sad tenderness and love for natural beauty. Moran loves the wild birds of his garden, and the most moving passage in the whole book is that describing how he returns home to find that his bees are now only a dry handful of dust of annulets and wings. We are told that Sapo loved nature, particularly the flight of the hawk, and felt joy at the strangeness and beauty of animals and plants; and many passages in Beckett's works, for example his account of the Lamberts' mule, reveal his deep feeling for animal life.

On the psychological level the three novels are a study of alternating or multiple personality involving mania, but deliberately omitting certain tracts of the protagonist's life. It is, for example, quite clear that he was a man of some learning: Molloy chooses to wrap himself in *The Times Literary Supplement*; Moran refers to Augustine and more obscure theologians; Malone mentions Tiepolo's ceiling at Würzburg; M. casually introduces Botal's Foramen into his monologue. But there is no account of his life between the teen-age of Sapo and the middle-age of Moran. One may assume that he studied at a university (like Murphy) and had travelled on the continent, say in his early twenties, but we are never given any account of this part of his life.

The work also has religious and mystical connotations, which have already been indicated. With these are involved all the scatological passages which are bound to offend so many readers. This arises out of the contrast between a dimly glimpsed transcendent Self (whether this is felt as a beatific vision or as a nirvana) and the concrete reality of what Pope called 'this disease, my life': a contrast so great and painful to certain religious temperaments (including many Christian saints) that this world only conjures up images of horror and filth in their minds.

On a philosophical level Descartes, as Professor Kenner has shown, has largely influenced Beckett's thought; but so also has Schopenhauer, and not merely because of his pessimism and sensitivity to the evil and suffering in life. In the early essay on

Proust (1931) Beckett interprets Proust's work, and in particular his treatment of music, specifically in the light of Schopenhauer's theory of Art; and I have already indicated the role played by the assertion and attempted denial of the will in *The Unnamable*.

Moreover the account of the Unnamable's vain search for his real 'me', which is predicated as the basis underlying his various vice-existers, exemplifies R. D. Laing's concept of 'ontological insecurity' as the root condition for the genesis of schizophrenia. Thus while the first two novels are concerned with psychotic symptoms and subjective experiences, the third novel probes more deeply into their cause.

# Six

# 'The Thing Itself'

As One Reads the novels in sequence one notes a tendency to deprive the protagonist more and more of possessions and attributes which are not essential to the central core of a human being. Murphy abandoned his bourgeois social position and practically all his possessions, except the rocking chair which helped him to close his eyes to the outer world and retire within his mind. Watt abolished the normal 'real' world and lived a life of phantasy. Moran, living at first an inhibited, methodical, middle-class life, bounded by his possessions, house and garden, was driven by his voices to abandon all and wander into the 'Molloy country', where that physical deterioration commenced which ended in Molloy with his two stiff legs and his lack of toes. Molloy's possessions, like Malone's, were reduced to a minimum, a few intrinsically worthless remnants which, nevertheless, had value for their possessor. And in Mahood we reach the limit of denudation; a trunk and head, limbless, with no possessions and no power of speech. Thus reduced he seems as close to 'unaccommodated man' as he could possibly be and yet live.

Yet Beckett goes further, and deprives his protagonist, M, of the whole physical body and of all perception of, and relationship with, the external physical world. But M, still animated by the Will, is impelled to clothe his essential Self with images, the last of which is Worm. To realize Worm imaginatively he necessarily has to attribute to it some signs of existence, such as hearing or movement; but these immediately negate it as a transcendent being; they are 'lendings' which obscure 'the thing itself'. There is no issue from this impasse.

In 1950 Beckett wrote *Textes Pour Rien* (*Texts for Nothing*, included now in *No's Knife*), a series of short monologues by a schizophrenic tramp who is baffled by the problem of self. He does not know what he is, nor whether he is, but would 'like to be sure I left no stone unturned before reporting me missing, and giving up.' These texts contain many striking passages but are mainly variations on the themes of the *Trilogy* with some anticipations of those in his next novel, *Comment C'est* (1960) which appeared in 1964 in English as *How It Is*. To this we must now turn.

In *How It Is* Beckett tries once more to present an existence stripped of all 'lendings', but from quite a different angle. Here we have the underlying psi-component undergoing an infinite series of births and re-births separated by purgatorial intervals, and there is no sign of a beginning nor of an end to this chain of re-incarnations. The book is divided into three parts: Before Pim (The Journey), With Pim (The Couple) and After Pim (The Abandon). These represent three links in the chain, the middle one being a period of incarnate human life, and the first and last the periods of discarnate life. It is an extraordinary picture of a being, some sort of self, endowed with a kind of image-body, existing in darkness face down on a sea of mud. This being is referred to as 'I' or 'me' and seems to correspond to the M. of *The Unnamable*.

In Parts One and Three there is no direct experience of human life on earth, but only 'bits and scraps' of memories which are 'ill-captured'. But in Part Two (With Pim) there seems to be an interaction between 'I' and Pim which parallels at a deep level of the psyche the interaction taking place on earth between the ego, or superficial personality, and other people. In addition there are various little scenes, or images, of earth-life reported by Pim to 'me'.

# 1 The Journey

In Part One (Before Pim) he is crawling over the mud towards Pim. He is alone, and has a sack full of tins of food, fortunately with a tin-opener also, to sustain him. He hears a voice, which once was external but now is inside him, telling him scraps of his past life though now it is only to be heard 'when the panting stops'. One remembers that Molloy panted, and that Moran said of him: 'He had only to rise up within me for me to be filled with panting.' And Molloy, too, crawled and dragged himself through the forest in a way very similar to that described here:

'. . . throw the right hand forward bend the right knee these joints are working the fingers sink the toes sink in the slime these are my holds . . . push pull the leg straightens the arm bends all these joints are working the head arrives alongside the hand flat on the face and rest.' There is no punctuation, and this makes some of the passages difficult to decipher with certainty, though the above passage presents no difficulty.

The voice recalls to him 'bits and scraps' of memories and images of his previous life on earth; they are 'ill-said ill-heard ill-recaptured ill-murmured in the mud'. He cannot speak but only make 'brief movements of the lower face'. He believes that somewhere, somehow his life has been recorded, that someone listens and makes notes; but he is also sceptical about having ever really lived on earth:

'life life the other above in the light said to have been mine on and off no going back up there no question no one asking that of me never there a few images on and off in the mud earth sky a few creatures in the light some still standing.'

And he drops the subject to attend to something he is certain about, the sack with its tins. He considers emptying them all out and then putting them back, but fears to lose some in the mud; then he contemplates opening one to eat something, say tunny. Apart from the sack and tins he can only be certain of the mud, darkness, silence and solitude.

As he crawls slowly along, through a vast stretch of time, various images of fragmentary memories of his previous life arise. The first one is of some creature whom he watches, as in a mirror, saying that he is better than he used to be, but adding that he himself (the narrator) goes steadily from bad to worse. Presumably this 'creature' was in fact himself. Then occurs another image, of himself as an infant, and shortly after this a third, of a woman sewing and looking at him while he sits silent with his head and hand on a table.

In order to drag himself along more easily he ties the sack with a cord round his neck leaving both hands free. He reflects that here there are no others to call on him and talk about themselves, and so no stories but what he can tell himself. As a distraction, when dreams and images and food fail, he can only pull back his hand and wave it in front of his face.

Soon he sees another image, of himself in infancy saying his prayers at his mother's knee, and gazing into her face.

'We are on a veranda smothered in verbena the scented sun dapples the red tiles . . . the huge head hatted with birds and flowers is bowed down over my curls the eyes burn with severe love . . . in a word bolt upright on a cushion on my knees whelmed in a nightshirt I pray according to her instructions.'

F

'that's not all she closes her eyes and drones a snatch of the so-called Apostles' Creed I steal a look at her lips

'she stops her eyes burn down on me again I cast up mine and repeat awry'

That this particular image is derived from Beckett's own childhood memories is revealed by a charming photograph (reproduced in *Beckett at Sixty*) which shows the infant Sam, perhaps two years old, saying his prayers at his mother's knee. She is seated against a brick wall and wearing an outdoor coat and a large hat with some trimming; as the photograph cuts off half this hat one cannot see any birds or flowers on it. The shadows and some fogging on the edge of the picture suggest that it was taken in bright sunshine, not in an enclosed room, and one can just see that the floor is tiled—we are obviously on the veranda of the house. Sam himself kneels upright on a cushion, 'whelmed in a nightshirt' which spills out over his feet, while his mother bends down over him. Thus, apart from the verbena and the colour of the tiles, the details of the photograph reproduce the 'image' exactly. Of course the emotional overtones in the passage quoted should not be attributed to the child in so lucid a form—they are the adult author's elaboration of vague feelings of awe and anxiety remembered from infancy.

He continues crawling while reflecting that these images are false, that he is not like that any more, and he notices that his tins have suddenly dwindled to half what they were at first so that he may soon be left with the empty sack. He talks soundlessly to the sack, moving his lower jaw for the words and, feeling the need of a witness (as Mr Knott did), he conjures up Kram who bends over him, shining his lamp on him, and reports the words to his aide Krim who enters them in a ledger.

After another 'image', of a crocus in a pot held up in the sunlight by a hand, he begins to wonder how he got here, and to reflect on the theme of reincarnation. 'you are there somewhere alive somewhere vast stretch of time then its over you are there no more alive no more then again you are there again alive again it wasn't over an error you begin again.'

He begins to look forward to the approaching period 'with Pim' and then the one 'after Pim' and after these, he hopes, it should be an eternal rest with no more journeys, couples, or abandons. And at last he articulates a sound 'aha, signifying mamma', a barely audible sound, as much as he can manage with his mouth open, but hinting at his approaching rebirth into the world, which corresponds to his time with Pim.

So he crawls on hoping for night when he can sleep and on waking reach Pim. He thinks of eating and finds there are only a dozen tins left. and after a few pages of random reflections on his situation he suddenly feels that the end of the journey is imminent. But he has not arrived yet; another image intervenes, of a boy sitting on his satchel with his back against a wall, looking up at the sky, and dreaming that he sees Jesus. When this image disappears he crawls a few yards and reaches a precipice, over which he falls clutching his now empty sack.

All the tins are gone now, but he comforts himself for a moment with the thought that in this period, Part One, he has not been given the torment of having tins but no opener, nor an opener without tins, as might conceivably have been his lot. Nevertheless he feels he must look for tins; though his own have disappeared into the mud behind him perhaps if he goes on in a zig-zag path each side of his destined straight-line he will come across some half-empty tins thrown away by others who have preceded him, or even perhaps 'a celestial tin miraculous sardines sent down by God at the news of my mishap.' But after a few yards progress his hand suddenly clutches at the rump of Pim and he has reached his immediate goal: 'the hand dips clawing for the take instead of the familiar slime an arse two cries one mute end of Part One before Pim that's how it was before Pim.'

## 2 The Couple

Part Two (With Pim) is concerned with the manner in which he makes Pim his witness, trains him first to speak and answer questions, and then makes him tell of his life 'above in the light'— but though ostensibly it is Pim's life that is being related it is apparently also 'mine'. It is 'my' task to give life to Pim, who without 'me' lies inert in the mud. But the distinction between 'me' and Pim is apt to get blurred so that many of the passages are ambiguous in their attribution, especially since at one point, when he gives Pim his name, he also claims that his own name is Pim too. In fact, Pim is really the incarnated 'me'.

When his hand first descended upon Pim it instantly recoiled, and then settled firmly down with a sense of ownership, and he dug his nails into the flesh of Pim's backside, eliciting a cry of fright. Thus assured that Pim is a living creature he now has the task of making him articulate and responsive, so that he can report on the life above, on earth. This training is arduous and, for Pim, painful and it takes vast stretches of time. It starts after an initial, relatively happy period, during which the two simply rest lying side by side. The mere presence of another being is comforting even without any communication between them, at least for a while.

At some point Pim suddenly sings a tune and this shows that he could be made to speak. So a ruthless process of training on Pavlovian lines is started. In order to provoke the singing he digs his nails into Pim's armpit; when Pim cries he gets a thump on the head which pushes his face into the mud. This is repeated until at last, Pim, having racked his brains to guess what his tormentor wants, instead of crying sings. When it is sufficiently established that nails in the armpit are a command to sing the next thing is to make him speak. For this it is first necessary to delve into Pim's sack for a tin-opener, with which he can jab Pim in the buttocks as a stimulus. Naturally the jabs only produce more cries at first, which are followed by thumps on the skull, until poor Pim, reasoning that his master must be demanding something that is not beyond his powers to give, and that neither singing nor crying is the right response, finally murmurs something unintelligible. After endless repetitions a code is evolved and learnt till the responses follow the stimuli mechanically. Once this is accomplished the next task is to teach Pim to answer when questions are written on his back by scratching words in capital letters with the finger-nails. This too takes ages, but at last Pim responds and is made to recount scraps from his life above in the light; but whether what he says under this torture is real or invented there is no knowing: 'that life then said to have been his invented remembered a little of each no knowing that thing above he gave it me I made it mine what I fancied skies especially.'

The 'I' no longer sees the images that he saw in Part One, but instead Pim sees little scenes and reports them to him, but it seems to be the same human existence in both cases. Eventually however he runs out of questions and Pim out of answers about this life above, and so he tries to make Pim tell him about his (Pim's) life in the mud before they came together, particularly whether he heard a voice in that period; but this only produces utter confusion and no response can be got from Pim, who is unaware of discarnate existence, being only conscious of the 'life in the light.'

This attempt having failed, it only remains to make Pim tell more about his life above, and this produces a moving picture of his wife's death—but is it Pim's wife or his? 'samples my life above Pim's life we're talking of Pim my life up there my wife.' The ambiguity is deliberate, for 'I' and Pim are two portions of the same self. His wife broke her back falling, or jumping, from a window.

We glean a picture of his parents, the father, perhaps a builder, killed by falling off the scaffolding; his mother holding her bible with her finger marking the place, '. . . psalm one hundred and something oh God man his days as grass,' and of himself: 'never good at anything not made for that farrago too complicated crawl about in corners and sleep all I wanted I got it nothing left but to go to heaven.' It is Sapo and Macmann over again, unable to cope with the demands of society, opting out of the struggle.

A long time goes by with Pim silent, while Kram and Krim bend down thinking perhaps he is now dead; but no, they prod him and he renews his scenes of life. The first scene harks back to one of the images of Part One: a boy 'ten or twelve years old, sleeping in the sun at the foot of the wall'—it is the same who dreamt that he saw Jesus 'with a golden goatee clad in an alb.' After this a scene of himself in the stern of a boat sailing at night in moonlight towards some island, which might perhaps relate to a reference, made a few pages later, to 'up the gangways between decks with emigrants.'

He starts to write E.N.D. in capitals on Pim's back, but is checked by another memory or image, of himself aged fifty, sixty, or eighty, kneeling on straw, in a stable, with a dog beside him, praying hopelessly. 'there I am again how I last on my knees hands joined before my face thumb-tips before my nose finger tips before the door my crown or vertex against the door one can see the attitude not knowing what to say whom to implore what to implore no matter it's the attitude that counts the intention.'

This baffled old man, praying a 'prayer without words against a stable-door,' longing for release, might be Malone again in a depressive phase regressing back to the boy in his nightshirt praying uncomprehendingly according to his mother's instructions.

Pim is now subjected to a whole series of questions from which it appears that he has no idea how he got here but thinks he was always in the mud, had never experienced any voice or contact with another person, sees occasional scenes but has no memories, nothing to prove that he ever lived up there, cannot either affirm or deny anything; he wishes to die but does not expect to. Under pressure, for the sake of peace, he admits that there was a life before the other, with the other, after the other but he can't describe it; and then Pim departs, leaving 'me' alone in the mud.

Part Two expands an obscure passage in *The Unnamable*: 'He'll come and lie on top of me, lie beside me, my dear tormentor, his turn to suffer what he made me suffer, mine to be at peace.' The inner self of the split personality forces the other portion (Pim) to communicate his experiences of other people in 'the life above'. As the personalities alternate so their roles are interchanged and Pim (now called Bom) becomes the tyrant.

Thus there should be two episodes of 'the couple', i.e. an extra Part Four with Bom; but the second couple is an exact replica of the first one, because it is merely the identical mutual interaction between self and others only looked at from the opposite point of view. Part Two is active, my action on Pim; Part Four would be passive, Bom's action on me: but Pim and Bom are the same person in the final analysis, and both are really aspects of 'me'.

After the death of the physical body (i.e. when Pim departs, or when 'I' leave Bom) my psi-component is left discarnate, and this period (a vast stretch of time) is also described from two points of view. The first is Part One, the journey, when I am impelled towards re-birth, which is interpreted as my long crawl towards Pim. The second, the abandon, will constitute Part Three. In this period I seem to be inert in the mud, greatly concerned to interpret and explain my past experiences, of which a few scraps of memory remain. But the journey and the abandon, Parts One and Three, are really the same period of discarnate existence, regarded first as that before the next incarnation and then as that after the previous one. Actually this has already been intimated in Part One, where he interrupts the sequence of the narrative to say: 'this voice once quaqua then in me when the panting stops Part Three after Pim not before not with I have journeyed found Pim lost Pim it is over I am in Part Three after Pim how it was. . . .'

Scattered through Parts One and Two there are various fragmentary glimpses of childhood, and these, together with a few which occur in the *Trilogy*, may enable us to form a picture of the boy who began life as Sapo and died as Malone.

The very earliest recollection is one of 'old men how they dandled me on their knees little bundle of swaddle and lace.' This is a curious memory to retain from infancy, and one wonders who these old men were—perhaps the two grandfathers who might well have been doting and affectionate, whereas the parents were unsympathetic and stern. We may compare this 'image' with a comment by Molloy, 'I never really had much love to spare, but all the same I had my little quota, when I was small, and it went to the old men, when it could.'

In the 'image' of the perplexed boy kneeling and repeating his prayers at his mother's dictation he tells us that her eyes 'burn with severe love'—the significant adjective reveals the ambivalence of his feeling towards his mother. She, presumably, was responsible for the early religious training which clearly aroused a deep anxiety in the child, as is implied by the fact that in the 'image' of the boy dreaming that he meets Jesus he 'wakes up in a sweat.'

Malone refers once to his early childhood and gives the same impression of a total lack of comprehension between mother and son.

He was watching one of the first aeroplanes looping the loop, standing on a racecourse holding his mother's hand. She called it a miracle, on which he says: 'Then I changed my mind. We were not often of the same mind.' And when the boy asks her, 'without malice' (a revealing phrase!) how far away the sky really is, and she replies, 'to me, her son,' that it is exactly as far as it appears to be, her answer appals him.

It is obvious from these slight pictures that very early in his childhood this boy felt his mother to be a stranger whom he both loved and feared, and who was imcomprehensible to him. The estrangement from his parents is depicted more fully in the accounts of Moran's teen-age son and of Sapo. To Moran the motherless boy was a disobedient and thoroughly untrustworthy dolt, whom he treated with arbitrary and irrational severity; there was a total lack of mutual trust and sympathy between them.

Sapo, as recollected by Malone, is a dull, puzzled, harmless, schizoidal boy, quite out of touch with his petty-minded parents who assume, with no justification, that he will succeed in one of the learned professions, and are continually disappointed by his failure to learn anything.

Finally Mahood adds his quota to the portrait of the schoolboy in his fantasy of 'sitting among the children, babbling, cringing from the rod. I'll die in the lower third, bowed down with years and impositions.'

Altogether these disjointed glimpses of childhood add up to a composite picture of profound estrangement and lack of confidence between the boy and his parents and teachers, a condition which, because it engenders bewilderment and insecurity in the child, is typically favourable to the schizophrenic flight away from reality into phantasy.

## 3 The Abandon

Part Three, how it was after Pim, begins confusedly with attempts to recall the past before it all goes blank, but the result seems to be the conclusion that Pim 'never was only me me Pim how it was before me with me after me how it is'—in fact Pim was himself.

At this point he suddenly discovers a sack, the one which Pim has left behind, and this starts his imagination (which was on the decline, or spent, according to previous passages) so that he begins to create a body-image for himself: '. . . say you see it an arm colour of mud the hand in the sack quick say an arm then another.'

Here, as also happened in *The Unnamable*, we have gone back to primitive magic, the belief in the omnipotence of words; it is sufficient to say 'arm' for there to be an arm, not, of course, in physical reality, but at least in the image-world of discarnate existence—'in the beginning was the word.'

Soon his voice, which was silent in Part Two, comes back again, and he also begins to hear another voice, or voices, which tell him things about himself, and give him the words in which he can formulate it all. And so he is led on to recollections of previous states, as for example the one before Part One, when Bem (name for the previous appearance of Bom) tormented him just as he tormented Pim. Bem eventually was left abandoned, because the narrator set off on the journey towards Pim. But at this point a difficulty occurs: how do we account for the sack which he had in Part One? He must have left his own sack with Bem, just as Pim left his at the end of Part Two. Yet he had a sack on the journey, so where did it come from? Obviously he must have found it ready waiting for him to come and pick it up. But this involves there being a sack ready for each one of the million souls at each of the innumerable places where they start on a journey; and as one person's cycle of journey, couple, abandon, couple, is repeated throughout eternity there must be an infinite number of sacks already laid out on a line for each one of us.

This leads him to long and complex efforts to work out the sequence of events, but the difficulties of an infinite series along a straight line are too great; though if one considered a closed circle, so that there would be no first or last involved, things would be simpler. However, in spite of the fact that one can make a fairly simple scheme involving only four persons working round a circle, he rejects the idea, being convinced that circular motion only holds for the earth, and that here in the mud motion in a straight line is the rule. From this, on the assumption that justice prevails, he decides that there must be an infinite number of souls pursuing an infinite series of states; for otherwise there would be one at the beginning deprived of his tormentor and one at the end without his victim. So the only possible alternatives seem to be either that there is an infinite number of souls, or that he is totally alone and that Pim and Bom are creatures of his imagination.

And he goes on to consider, through many pages, the various infinitudes involved in the conception of the procession. He gets entangled in the problem of what would happen to the narrative if he had begun with the couple (Part Two) instead of the journey (Part One), and he concludes that only three of the four episodes are communicable, since Part Four (with Bom) is identical with Part Two, Pim and Bom being two names for the same being: '. . . the two couples that in which I figure in the north as tormentor and that in which I figure in the south as victim compose the same spectacle exactly.'

Then another difficulty arises over the sacks; for an infinite number of souls journeying along a straight line and passing an infinite number of halting places (at Parts Two and Four) would require there to be an infinite number of sacks piled up at each halt—and how then could the procession ever get moving? Like Voltaire, he sees the necessity of inventing God to remove this difficulty: '. . . if we are to be possible our couplings journeys and abandons need of one not one of us an intelligence somewhere a love who all along the track at the right places according as we need them deposits our sacks.'

And it is reasonable to attribute exceptional powers to this beneficent being, so perhaps it is he who listens and notes things down, not Kram, and it may be his voice that is heard telling me of my life above; in fact 'the voice of him who before listening to us murmur what we are tells us what we are as best he can.'

But God might well wonder if all these histories are worth while, and he might decide to stop the sequence of journeys, leaving us permanently in one state. Consider the possibility that we are all glued together in one mass, so that each is at the same time Pim and Bom, at once speechless and speaking! But detailed examination of this leads to difficulties, as each would have to speak or sing at the same time as his face would be pushed into the mud by his tormentor. Alternatively God might stop the procession at the season of the couples, in which case one half of the souls would be victims for ever and the other half tormentors, which is manifestly unjust. On the other hand, if it were stopped at the season of journeys and abandons, although everyone would be at peace still injustice would prevail, since half would be deprived of a victim who is their due, and the others would lack the tormentor who should be coming to them.

Since none of these speculations give him a satisfactory solution to the problem of existence he harks back to the simplest solution, namely that only he himself exists, and the whole series of journeys, couples, abandons, with Pim, Bom, Kram, God are just creations of his own imagination. We are back in the old solipsism which began in *Murphy*. Still there is some external reality, the mud, the dark, in addition to himself with his voice and the panting, so the solipsism is not quite one hundred per cent —indeed in practice it never can be; even inside an asylum the solipsist draws a line somewhere.

He has never journeyed, or suffered, or been abandoned, nor was there anyone listening to or noting his murmurs; and his voice, he tells himself, will get less and less, so he reasons that change is possible, and thus death is also possible. He puts the questions to himself, and it is his voice that answers or refuses to answer: 'so things may change no answer end no answer I may choke no answer . . . trouble the peace no more no answer the silence no answer die no answer Die screams I MAY DIE screams I SHALL DIE screams good.'

As is inevitable, there are no answers to the fundamental questions, but their urgency is revealed by the screams.

We have reached the end of 'how it was after Pim how it is' and finished a Pilgrim's Progress that would have appalled Bunyan. Is the work properly to be called a novel? Or is it rather to be classed as a Prophetic Book, like *Jerusalem*? Personally I don't see that the question is of the least importance, any more than it is in the case of *Finnegans Wake*; both books are half prose, half poetry, epical in character, and full of difficulties for the reader, and both repay, indeed they demand, repeated reading and close study.

While it is obvious that Beckett is the true successor of Joyce, with whom he was well acquainted, there is little similarity between their ideas or styles or temperaments. Joyce came from a Catholic home and was educated by Jesuits, whereas Beckett was brought up as a strict Protestant. Both men rebelled against their religious upbringing, yet their works are permeated by religious symbols and ideas. But Joyce was fundamentally an optimist, a life worshipper, whereas Beckett's work is deeply pessimistic and coloured by his feeling of horror and pity for the indignities and sufferings of humanity. Each refers frequently to the Fall, but in Joyce this evokes the response 'O Felix Culpa', while for Beckett it signifies 'the crime of having been born.' There is a world of difference between the picture of Eternal Recurrence painted by Joyce, for example in the transformations of Nuvoletta, falling as a 'singult tear' becoming 'wiggly livvly', then 'gossipacious Anna Livia', and finally the old Anna Livia going back, sad and weary, to her father the ocean; between this picture and that painted by Beckett, of a lost soul struggling along a sea of mud, impelled to re-incarnate in an infinite series of pseudo-personalities who pant with frustration. In spite of trials and tribulations Earwicker's Viconian cycle contains the joy of life which is absent from the unending series of journeys, couples, and abandons endured by Pim.

# Seven

# 'All White in the Whiteness'

BECKETT'S NEXT PROSE WORK, *Imagination Dead Imagine** (1966), is described as a novel, though I would say that it can more fitly be called a prose-poem. It is true that there are two people in it, but they lie motionless and do not communicate; there are also a few events, such as changes from hot to cold, light to dark, and stillness to vibration. But the only event that could be called an action consists of the opening of one eye by each of the 'non-characters'. Under these circumstances the term 'novel' seems a misnomer.

The work commences by the author first denying that imagination is dead, and then conceding that you may suppose it to be so. Significantly, the immediate result is that the external world, earth, sea and sky, disappear too, for they (as Schopenhauer said) are 'my idea', i.e. an imaginative construction. Nevertheless, the author at once imagines an internal world: a closed white rotunda suspended in a shining white vacuum. He gives us the exact measurements, diameter three feet, total height three feet, wall eighteen inches high; although the significance of these figures is obscure the fact that they are not surds suggests that we are still in a rational domain.

On the floor of the rotunda, packed tightly each within a semi-circle, a man and a woman lie back to back and head to tail, with their legs drawn up so that knees and feet touch the wall, reminding one of a foetus in the womb. They lie quite still, on their right sides, occasionally opening the left eye to stare unwinking in the white light. Apart from this, and the facts that they breathe faintly and also sweat, they might be dead. They say nothing and do nothing, but if you were to break the silence even with a murmur of 'ah' they would react with an 'infinitesimal shudder instantaneously suppressed.'

Inside the rotunda all is at first heat and whiteness; there is no

* Now included in *No's Knife*.

external source of light, but everything radiates. However, this state is not permanent, for there is a persistent alternation between heat and cold, light and darkness. Sometimes the regularity of the changes is broken by pauses or even by reversals of direction, at intermediate levels, and when this happens there is a turmoil of vibration. Calm is restored only when the extreme of light (or of darkness) is reached and a pause occurs before the next change begins. These calm interludes seem to correspond with the pre-natal and post-mortem states, while the 'agitated light' of the transitional periods corresponds to 'Life's fitful fever' in successive reincarnations.

This short, highly symbolical work is a kind of pendant to *How It Is*, or perhaps a supplement to it, presenting another aspect of 'unaccommodated man' deprived now, not of all bodily substance, but of the ultimate 'lending', imagination. Most of the symbolism has already been present in the previous novel, where (in Part Three) we find also the idea of the title, in the references to 'imagination spent' and 'imagination on the decline'. The vibration and stillness are prefigured by 'the panting' and 'when the panting stops'. The alternations between whiteness and darkness are paralleled by the states 'above in the light.' and 'the dark the mud.' The rotunda, symbol both of the skull and the womb, is there too: '. . . the little vault empty closed eight planes bone-white if there were a light a tiny flame all would be white.' This vault, elsewhere called a rotunda, is the skull in which imagination dwells. In *Imagination Dead Imagine* there is no voice, and no tiny flame, but the rotunda itself radiates whiteness and exists in an empty white radiance which inevitably recalls Shelley's 'white radiance of eternity'; though for Beckett life does not stain it with many colours, but throws it into a state of agitated vibration.

The multiple symbolism of this rotunda includes not only the unending cycle of re-incarnations and the ebb and flow of consciousness inside the skull, but also, and perhaps more importantly, the intra-uterine stage in man's life. The foetal position, the rhythmic alternations of temperature, the hardly perceptible breathing and the profound quiescence suggest the life within the womb. The previous novels have contained many womb symbols and it is obvious that Beckett attaches great importance to this theme. The statement by Peggy Guggenheim (in her *Confessions of an Art Addict*) that 'Ever since his birth Beckett had retained a terrible memory of life in his mother's womb. He was constantly suffering from this and had awful crises, when he felt he was suffocating.' is obviously highly relevant here. Some people may doubt the possibility of such a memory and class it as a later construction of the mind; but this in no way diminishes its importance. What seems rather odd, however, is that in the novels the womb-life is considered a state to be desired—to Molloy it was the only 'just endurable' part of his existence; Murphy, Watt, and Moran in their different ways try to approximate to this state of warmth, torpor, and insulation from external stimuli. It seems more likely that this 'terrible memory' was really that of being ejected from the womb, not of the life within it. The feeling of suffocation, mentioned by Peggy Guggenheim, supports this view, and also may explain why Molloy and Pim both panted so insistently.

An interesting point of difference between this new work and the previous novels is that here there is a woman as well as a man, the two together being treated as one unit within the rotunda. Beckett seems to be adopting the modern view that biologically and psychologically man is a bisexual being, as Plato long ago depicted him in his myth of the original Androgyne. Or perhaps it is only that he is giving belated recognition to the importance of woman, for in all the previous novels women play only very minor and incidental roles and, with the one exception of Murphy's Celia, are either comic or horrible caricatures. Even Molloy's mother, whose influence over him was crucial, and whom one might expect to be portrayed in some detail, is only presented to us as what Shelley might have described as 'an old, mad, blind, despised and dying'—hag. Not until *How It Is* do we get a glimpse of her in her younger days, in the 'image' where she teaches the boy his prayers. In the plays after *Godot* and *Endgame* women appear as major characters; Mrs Rooney and Winnie are very real people, and even the unnamed First Woman and Second Woman in *Play* are individuals, not pasteboard figures. It is somewhat remarkable that there should be this great difference between his presentation of women in the twenty years from *Murphy* to *Endgame* and that in the eight years from *All That Fall* to *Play*.

# Ping

In *The Unnamable* we had the post-mortem self depicted as still the creature of will and imagination, so that although M. yearned for annihilation and 'the true silence' when he should have spoken the right words which would release him, nevertheless he could not escape from words and images and so he had to 'go on'.

Some ten years later, in *How It Is*, Beckett returned to this theme, but gave a different picture, of a post-mortem self undergoing an unending series of incarnations. Here imagination still persists, though more fitfully, and it endows Pim with a shadowy kind of body, to say nothing of the sack and tins. The blind will to live also operates here as well as the longing for release. Pim's reflections on his existence lead to the solipsistic conclusion that only he is real and all his experiences are imaginary; and the book ends with his hysterical desperate assertion that death must finally annihilate him for ever.

Neither Worm nor Pim was quite satisfactory as a portrait of 'the thing itself', and in *Imagination Dead Imagine* Beckett has made a new attempt. The two in the rotunda are bereft of will and of imagination; therefore bereft also of ideas, words and percepts. They are not conscious, like Neary, of 'the big blooming buzzing confusion' or, like Moran, 'drowned in a spray of phenomena'. But they have bodies and dwell in a solid rotunda of definite dimensions. Beckett reached a limit when he had stripped the self down to imagination and will.

But Beckett always seems able to take another step forward when one thinks that he has reached the limit. He is able to give the old *motifs* new expression in unexpected ways, usually involving a more condensed, therefore more obscure, style which makes greater demands on the reader's intuition. Certainly this is so with the short piece called *Ping* which first appeared (in English) in the February 1967 number of *Encounter* and now is included in *No's Knife*.

The limbo depicted here is somewhat similar to that in *Imagination Dead*, only instead of the rotunda with its two inert bodies we have a shining white room, one yard square by two yards high, in which a white naked body is fixed, his legs joined as if sewn together and only the pale blue eyes perhaps capable of movement. I cannot accept the suggestion of David Lodge (in *Encounter*, January 1968) that this is a dying man *in extremis*, for the whole set-up is obviously symbolical and it would be ridiculous to imagine a dying man standing naked and rigid in such a box, which is clearly a variant of the white rotunda. As a post-mortem limbo, however, it is no less acceptable than Pim's sea of mud or the Unnamable's empty dark space.

This body has minute traces of consciousness, not of sensations received from outside, but of dim images arising from memory—signs without meaning and just perceptible murmurs, and faint

colours, blue, grey and rose, which immediately fade into white
and so are indistinguishable from the white room. This consciousness seems to be switched on and off by *Ping*, a vibration (presumably internal?) which has a similar function to that of the spotlight in *Play* and the Opener in *Cascando*. There are moments when
the creature seems to be 'fixed' elsewhere but really is 'always
there but that known not,' and the final words 'ping silence ping
over' suggest that Beckett now rejects the unending persistence
implied in the Unnamable's 'I'll go on,' and the eternal recurrence
of *How It Is*, in favour of the view that the psi-component fades
away eventually.

In *The Unnamable* the surviving psi-component was conceived
as having an extensive vocabulary and the ability to comment at
great length on his 'delusive quasi-perceptual experience.' When
writing *How It Is* some ten years later Beckett adopted a different
style in which short verse-like paragraphs reproduced a spasmodic, disjointed flow of ideas and images that suggested a much
more limited consciousness. But although punctuation is absent
there are still brief sentences with subject and main verb, and Pim
indulges in long chains of reasoning. But in *Ping* the expression is
vastly more condensed in order to capture the kind of primitive
image-thinking which might characterize the post-mortem state
of what C. D. Broad called the 'quasi-personal dream-like stream
of experience.' The meagre content of the consciousness, its ob-
sessional nature and its frustrations are conveyed by a small number of very short phrases without subjects or verbs, conjunctions
or commas; there is a sense of striving to attain a clear perception
of something but it only achieves a faint image '. . . a little less dim
eye black and white half closed long lashes imploring'—this seems
to be the utmost that can be recalled of, presumably, the girl he
had once loved. Does the word *imploring* imply that like Krapp and
Joe he also had rejected her?

Throughout the series of novels there is an interior sequence,
not that of the actual order of composition, but one which constitutes the saga of the schizophrenic M. Starting life as the apathetic
schizoidal boy Sapo, he went to college and then, a young man
calling himself Murphy, went to London where he opted out of
the middle-class rat race and tried to live in phantasy. In 1938
Beckett mistakenly thought he had finished with Murphy, so he
allowed him to die in his garrett. Next, he portrayed the full-
blown psychotic, Watt, who is what Murphy would have become
if he hadn't been gassed.

A few years later Beckett conceived the saga in which the course of the psychosis is delineated from the restricted, pre-psychotic personality of Moran, via his fugue, the acute catatonia of Molloy and the stuporose state of Macmann, to the senile dementia of Malone. In order to complete the picture he portrayed the boyhood of M. as Sapo, and during the course of the *Trilogy* he implicitly co-opted Murphy and Watt as members of this complex psyche.

Malone's death is not the end of the saga, for a portion of the psyche, the Unnamable, survives, striving to make sense of it all by finding his real identity which lies behind all these 'delegates', so that he may attain peace. Alas, this psychic remnant has to struggle on through endless reincarnations separated by long periods of existence on a dark sea of mud; its name is now Pim. However its consciousness seems eventually to dwindle away almost to nothing, leaving *Ping*, a spasmodic, momentary vibration, the ultimate 'thing itself'.

PART 2

# The Plays

*But thought's the slave of life, and life's time's fool;*
*And time, that takes survey of all the world,*
*Must have a stop.*
                    *Henry IV. Part I. v.4.*

# *Eight*

# 'The Pseudocouple'

## Waiting for Godot

IN SUCCESSIVE NOVELS Beckett has portrayed various phases of a schizophrenic, treating each one separately under the names of Moran, Molloy, Sapo, Malone and Macmann. In *The Unnamable* he dealt with an even more disintegrated state which might be described, in William Blake's phrase, as one of 'chaotic non-entity'. But now, in the two plays *Waiting for Godot* and *Endgame* he seems to be treating simultaneously on the stage the two basic selves of the split mind, the inner-self and the pseudo-self, embodied in a pair of characters whose inter-relationship is ambivalent, being based on mutual antagonism and mutual dependence. Though constantly at loggerheads they are at bottom 'like to a double cherry, seeming parted, but yet an union in partition.'

Though they do not exactly correspond to any of the M-personae of the novels, they are like them in many points; they are dilapidated old men, tired of the complexities of living, isolated from the world of common sense, and given to telling themselves stories. They are occupied with the same themes and problems that haunt Malone and the rest.

Actually it seems that around 1944–5 Beckett had a whole host of new ideas which he tried to work out in a novel called *Mercier et Camier*, but this has not been published because it could not deal adequately with them. The story of their futile journey was developed and greatly expanded into *The Trilogy*, while the idea of presenting two characters who, as a later reference to them as a 'pseudo-couple' implies, are not really separate persons but two halves of one man, was independently developed into the play *Waiting for Godot*.

The peculiar kind of cross-talk between Mercier and Camier in the novel re-appears in the dialogue between the two tramps in the play. The play differs from the novel in one important point, namely that whereas Mercier and Camier finally part company the two tramps, in spite of frequent suggestions of parting, remain together at the end; as two halves of one mind they are indissolubly bound together.

*En attendant Godot* was written at about the same time as *The Trilogy*, and when produced in 1952 it brought Beckett international recognition. It was a highly original departure from all the previously accepted ideas of what a play is. On a bare stage, which has only a dead-looking tree on it, two disreputable tramps, Estragon and Vladimir, are waiting for a nebulous figure, Godot, whom they have never seen and who in fact never does come. But he is essential for them, as they apparently expect him to tell them the meaning of their existence on earth, and thus to justify it. Meanwhile they have to occupy their time with desultory conversation and trivial actions. Their scraps of dialogue are inconclusive and ambiguous, touching on most of Beckett's favourite themes but never settling anything definitely. There is no continuous development either of observable action or of a line of thought, and at the end of the play the tramps are just as they were at the beginning. The opening words 'Nothing to be done,' spoken by Estragon while struggling with his boot, summarize the whole situation. And the closing words, 'Yes, let's go' are followed by the stage direction *They do not move* to confirm the inaction.

It is obviously not easy to describe the course of a play in which 'Nothing happens. Nobody comes. Nobody goes. It's awful.' Actually three other characters do arrive and depart, but they belong to phantasy rather than reality, and such small action as there is in the play is symbolical rather than meaningful in the sense of leading to any result. Some of it, indeed, such as the play with the hats or the struggles with a boot, seems merely to serve the purpose of holding the audience's attention.

Estragon, who was once a poet, is predominantly the withdrawn inner self. On the stage he several times attempts to go to sleep and dream; when woken up by Vladimir he loses his temper and with a gesture towards the universe exclaims 'This one is enough for you?' He has given up the struggle ('Nothing to be done'), and twice he suggests that they both hang themselves; in fact we learn that years ago he tried to drown himself in the Rhône but Vladimir rescued him. The suicidal impulses of the inner self are often countered by the pseudo-self which is more closely identified with the body than is the other; another example being

Molloy's ineffective attempt by slashing his wrists. In his role as the inner self we find that Estragon is the cold member of the pair, who refuses the embrace of his more warm-hearted companion and is generally more surly and even occasionally cruel. His contributions to the dialogue are apt to be terse, shrewd and gloomy, but sometimes he bursts out furiously and shouts with no apparently adequate provocation. Several times he suggests going away and separating from Vladimir, but actually he clings to his friend whose presence he needs—in fact they could not exist apart for long; as single cherries they would rot immediately.

Apparently, however, they do lose each other each night (when the body-bound pseudo-self sleeps) and during the day (when the pseudo-self is occupied with the outer world) and only come into communication during the twilight of evening. For both acts start in the evening, when they find each other after having each thought they had lost the other. Vladimir is joyous at their reunion and wants to embrace his friend, but Estragon is sulky. It seems that once again unknown persons have beaten him during the night; the life of the inner self in the periods when it is completely divorced from the pseudo-self is not the cosy state which Murphy found 'so pleasant that pleasant was not the word,' but is unfortunately likely to consist of terrifying phantasies.

Vladimir is more emotional, more easily hurt, and more dependent on friendship than is Estragon. He is also rather more hopeful, not quite convinced that there is 'nothing to be done'. He is the relatively practical one who suggests doing things to pass the time, provides carrots for Estragon to eat, notices in Act 2 that the tree now has leaves whereas the evening before it was quite bare, and keeps on reminding Estragon that they must stay there and wait for Godot. Vladimir, too, is the one who has a sense of time; he remembers when they worked together in the Macon country and he knows what day of the week it is, Saturday, and what they did yesterday evening. Estragon has very little sense of time and hardly any memory; he thinks it may be any old day of the week, and when asked about what was said at the beginning of this very evening can only reply 'Don't ask me. I'm not a historian.'

Still, conformably with his function of pseudo-self, Vladimir has a certain superstitious and vague feeling about religion. He suggests 'suppose we repented', and when Estragon asks 'Repented what?' he replies: 'Oh. . . . We wouldn't have to go into the details.' He is greatly interested in the fact that only one of the four Evangelists records that one of the thieves was saved; of the

others two do not mention the robbers at all, and the third implies
that both were damned. Vladimir is very worried by the dis-
crepancy between the four accounts, for it adds to the existing
uncertainty of salvation through the arbitrary working of Grace
which was already implicit in St Augustine's text:

> Do not despair: One of the thieves was saved.
> Do not presume: One of the thieves was damned.

To Estragon, however, theological doctrines are an irrelevant
nonsense compared with the appalling fact of the crucifixion
itself. Later in the play he proposes to go barefoot, at which the
practical Vladimir protests:

VLADIMIR:    But you can't go barefoot!
ESTRAGON:    Christ did.
VLADIMIR:    Christ! What's Christ got to do with it? You're
             not going to compare yourself to Christ!
ESTRAGON:    All my life I've compared myself to him.
VLADIMIR:    But where he was it was warm, it was dry!
ESTRAGON:    Yes. And they crucified quick.

In this dialogue Estragon is not suffering from delusions of
grandeur, imagining himself the equal of Christ; he is revealing
that his whole life has been one long crucifixion. Beckett constantly uses the cross as a symbol of the agony of human life
rather than of redemption—in this play it appears on the stage as
a tree on which Estragon proposes they should hang themselves,
and behind which he tries in vain to hide and abandons with the
comment: 'Decidedly this tree will not have been of the slightest
use to us.'
    After this theological passage they have a desultory conversa-
tion about whether Godot is to be expected in this place and this
evening or not, and after a slight quarrel and a reconciliation
Estragon suggests that they hang themselves on the tree. He
wants Vladimir to try first, for if the bough were to break under
his weight no harm would have been done; whereas if the lighter
man (himself) were to go first and the bough held, it still might
break under Vladimir's weight, in which case poor Vladimir
would be left alive alone. But they don't really know for certain
which of them is the heavier, so they decide that it is safer to do
nothing but wait to hear what Godot has to offer them.

When the dialogue seems to have come to a stand-still there is a noisy interruption and a new pair of fantastic characters appears. First comes Lucky, a very decrepit old man weighed down with all the luggage he is carrying. He is being driven forward at the end of a rope by Pozzo who enters cracking a whip. Pozzo is a burly figure dressed in loud checks looking like a cross between a cartoonist's pictures of a bookmaker and a plutocrat. At first the two tramps think he might be Godot, but Pozzo announces his name in loud tones and evidently expects them to be deeply impressed by it.

Pozzo domineers over the abject Lucky, whom he addresses as 'Pig' or 'Hog', ordering him to hand him his overcoat, hold the whip, bring the stool, then the luncheon basket and so on. At each command Lucky has to put down the rest of the baggage and pick it all up again before the next order, sagging under the weight and sleeping on his feet in the intervals. Pozzo settles himself down comfortably and eats his lunch and finally smokes his pipe while Estragon and Vladimir inspect Lucky and wax indignant over Pozzo's callous treatment of him.

Estragon is vastly puzzled by the fact that Lucky stands holding his baggage instead of putting it down. Pozzo says that he does it only to impress his master and so make him change his mind about selling his slave in the market, as was his intention. But one is reminded of Watt standing at the door wondering whether to set down his bags and rest on a chair, and deciding against it:

'For the sitting down was a standing up again, and the load laid down another load to raise.'

There are many similarities between Lucky and Watt, for example his general state of stupor, the catatonic movements of his limbs when he dances, and the schizophrenic composition of the speech which he rattles off with all its repetitions of unfinished sentences and apparently disconnected trains of thought. So too there are some similarities between Pozzo and the pre-psychotic Moran, notably his egocentric attitude, his bullying of Lucky as Moran bullied his son, his constant concern with the time and his material prosperity. Both men are described eating a good lunch and they both differ from all the others in their attention to their dress and also in the fact that they smoke—Moran's cigar and Pozzo's pipe are strongly emphasized.

When Pozzo has finished his lunch and thrown away the chicken bones (which Estragon retrieves and gnaws hungrily) he indulges in some pompous talk and finally remarks that the best thing to do

with such a creature as Lucky would be to kill him. At this Lucky
weeps and Estragon goes up to wipe away his tears only to receive
a violent kick from Lucky who, as Pozzo had previously told us,
is vicious with strangers.

And now in a somewhat obscure discourse Pozzo reveals their
true relationship:

'Guess who taught me all these beautiful things. My Lucky. . . .
But for him all my thoughts, all my feelings would have been of
common things. Professional worries! Beauty, grace, truth of the
first water, I knew they were all beyond me. So I took a knock.
. . . That was nearly sixty years ago.'

At this point he calls attention to his own comparatively youth-
ful appearance (though he is completely bald) in contrast to the
aged Lucky with his long white hair.

But what was this 'knock' which he took sixty years ago?
Clearly it was the onset of a schizophrenic split in which the
imaginative part of himself, the function which William Blake
called the Poetic Genius, was shut off and made into a feeble inner
self, while the remainder of the ego built up a pseudo-self which
was occupied with material prosperity. As time went on the
pseudo-self grew more and more domineering, self-important,
and callous but also more unsure of itself; on the other hand the
inner self became more unreal and impoverished. All this is
symbolized by Pozzo's aggressive and pompous manner, his self-
satisfied air and of course the rope and whip and other parapher-
nalia, and by the stupor and decrepitude of the starved slave,
Lucky. The split as embodied in Estragon and Vladimir is not so
severe; they still retain feelings of affection for each other, come
together each evening for mutual support and are visibly human
beings who suffer. But Pozzo and Lucky represent a much more
radical split in which the elements of feeling and imaginative
thought have been suppressed and starved while a swollen ego
has successfully pursued selfish material ends.

But we immediately find that Pozzo is not at all so secure as he
seems, for he breaks down, sobbing that he cannot bear Lucky's
behaviour. 'He used to be so kind . . . so helpful . . . and entertain-
ing . . . my good angel . . . and now . . . he's killing me.' However,
he calms down again and soon begins to worry about the time,
lest he should fall behind his schedule. Vladimir casually remarks
that time has stopped, which elicits from Pozzo the protest:
'Whatever you like, but not that.' For to the outward looking
pseudo-self time, as measured by the clock, is indispensable for

life. Pozzo is the incarnation of material earthly life, and as such is 'time's fool', while Lucky illustrates the fact that 'Thought's the slave of life.' Hotspur's third dictum has already been anticipated by Vladimir's statement.

A page or two later we learn that Lucky used to think very prettily once, and soon at the command of Pozzo he demonstrates his ability with an amazing speech which he rattles off at top speed and which concludes in a crescendo of manic confusion. It is a wonderful piece of schizophrenic oratory, a torrent of broken sentences and repeated phrases which makes a stream of apparently comic nonsense. But it contains a perfectly sane exposition of the fundamental impasse that has baffled all the theologians—how to reconcile our instinctive belief in a transcendent and beneficent Divine power with the undeniable experience of evil and misery. This thread of the speech may be summarized as follows:

Given the existence of a personal God with white beard who loves us dearly (with some exceptions) and suffers with those whom ('for reasons unknown but time will tell') he has damned and plunged into hell; yet it is certain that man, both potential and actual, wastes and pines; in spite of all our science, medicine, sports and physical culture man shrinks and dwindles. In short, humanity suffers and we know not why.

This speech shows many of the technical characteristics of schizophrenic thought disorders, such as the frequent repetitions of phrases quite out of context, echolalia (as in 'Feckham Peckham Fulham Clapham' or 'apathia athambia aphasia'), and the combination of two mutually contradictory ideas, as for example his statement that God loves us dearly 'from the heights of divine apathia'—for the word signifies complete indifference and lack of feeling.

I do not think previous commentators have noticed the connection between this speech and the well-known poem *Hyperions Schicksalslied* by the German poet Hölderlin, the last verse of which reads:

*Es schwinden, es fallen*
*Die leidenden Menschen*
*Blindlings von einer*
*Stunde zur andern*
*Wie Wasser von Klippe*
*Zu Klippe geworfen,*
*Jahrlang ins Ungewisse hinab.*

(Suffering humanity decays and falls blindly from hour to hour, like water hurled from cliff to cliff year after year down into the uncertain.)

This poem evidently impressed Beckett deeply, for it is echoed by Watt who, on coming round after his accident in the station waiting-room, hears the fragments 'von Klippe zu Klippe . . . endlos . . . hinab.' Moreover in Act 2 of this play Estragon's nightmare is concerned with falling from a height which plausibly could be a cliff.

The essence of Lucky's speech is that man 'wastes and pines, shrinks and dwindles', and these four verbs are all translations of the German verb *schwinden*. The images in the poem are strewn through the speech in a typically schizophrenic manner (technically called asyndetic thought) by which the exact thought is not reproduced by the precise word but is conveyed approximately by a number of closely related words. Thus the image of water is replaced by 'the seas the rivers the great deeps'; and Hölderlin's cliffs are not mentioned, but instead we have 'the mountains' and 'the abode of stones'. Again, the idea of a fall into an abyss appears behind 'in the great deeps the great cold' and 'the great cold the great dark'. The schizophrenic is unable to hit the definite word or image but produces near misses which are clearly connected with the image, as in this example the ideas of great depth, cold and darkness are with the abyss. All these images, of course, are poured out higgledy-piggledy without any logical links so that the whole speech is disjointed.

In the final twelve lines of the speech a new image, the skull, occurs eight times although it has no apparent linkage with surrounding words like tennis, stones and Connemara; but of course it is the natural image for man's ultimate fate, the end product of his wasting, pining, shrinking and dwindling in spite of the Deity's love and the progress of science and physical culture.

By the end of his speech Lucky is raving and has to be overpowered, but he is successfully brought back to his former state of stupor and made to hold all the baggage. When Pozzo prepares to take his leave, he discovers, to his dismay, that his watch has disappeared; a symbolic event which foreshadows his oncoming disintegration, for time is of the essence of his contract with himself. However, he departs as he arrived, driving Lucky at the end of the rope and cracking his whip, leaving Estragon and Vladimir to reflect upon the diversion he has caused.

And now a voice calling 'Mister' is heard, and a boy runs on to

the stage. He is received with hostility from Estragon and gentle-
ness from Vladimir who elicits the fact that Mr Godot has sent
him with the message that he can't come today but will surely
come tomorrow. Evidently a similar message was sent yesterday,
by a similar boy, for Vladimir thinks it is the same one again. But
it was his brother, the one who minds the sheep and gets beaten,
whereas tonight's messenger minds the goats and is not beaten.
Having delivered his message he departs with Vladimir's instruction to tell Mr Godot that he has seen them.

Now the moon rises, night falls, and they must seek shelter.
Estragon harks back to the idea of suicide and decides to bring a
piece of rope tomorrow. Then he wonders if it wouldn't be best
for them to separate, but finally decides that it would be too late
for that now. The pair sit down and agree upon going; but they
don't move and the curtain falls.

Act 2 takes place on the next evening, the only visible change
in the scene being that the tree has four or five leaves on it and
Lucky's hat is on the ground where it fell. Vladimir is the first to
enter, singing the interminable song (analogous to the recurring
decimal in *Watt*) about the dog and his tombstone. Then Estragon
comes in looking miserable and once more repulses the emotional
Vladimir. But there is a subtle difference from the similar beginning of Act 1. This time Estragon shows his need of Vladimir
almost at once: 'Don't touch me! Don't question me! Don't speak
to me! Stay with me!' and after looking at each other for quite a
while they suddenly embrace. Vladimir reveals in three short
exclamations the happiness of seeing a friend, the neutral calm of
being one in a couple, and the misery of the isolated self:
'(Joyous) There you are again. . . . (Indifferently) There we are
again. . . . (Gloomy) There I am again.'

Estragon has again been beaten up during the night, and it also
appears that his memory has deteriorated and he has forgotten
about the incident with Pozzo and Lucky. After a few pages of
inconsequential dialogue, during which Vladimir produces and
Estragon rejects a radish, and it seems to be established that the
boots which Estragon left on the stage yesterday have been ex-
changed in the night for another pair, he remarks:

'We always find something, eh Didi, to give us the impression
that we exist?' This is a theme which Beckett later on developed
into a whole play, *Happy Days*.

Soon Estragon goes to sleep once more, and Vladimir tenderly
covers him with his own coat. But he awakes from a nightmare

which Vladimir will not allow him to relate, so that we only hear
'It was falling. . . . I was on the top of a . . .'—surely a faint echo
of Hölderlin's poem, for the word *cliff* suggests itself as an obvious completion of the second sentence, while the first recalls
'humanity falls'.

Vladimir notices Lucky's hat lying on the ground and after
some comic exchanges of hats finally puts it on his head, throwing
down his own. He tries, not very successfully, to imitate Lucky
with the baggage, and Lucky dancing, but fails completely to copy
him thinking, although the hat was what enabled Lucky to think.

Soon there occurs the second appearance of Pozzo and Lucky,
but they have changed considerably. No longer the self-assertive,
domineering master, Pozzo is a blind man led by, not driving,
Lucky, to whom he is attached by a much shorter rope.

On seeing the two tramps Lucky stops, Pozzo bumps into him,
and both fall to the ground and are unable to get up. Lucky lies
like one dead, but Pozzo groans and cries for help, while Estragon
and Vladimir watch and debate whether to assist them or not,
perhaps in the hope of getting some reward. Vladimir, waxing
rather eloquent under the influence of Lucky's hat, commences a
moral discourse on their duty to help the fallen, but he soon
wanders away from the point and on to the question of why they
are here and how they beguile the time 'to prevent our reason
from foundering' if indeed it has not already done so.

Eventually, after Pozzo has offered them five shillings, Vladimir
attempts to pull him up, but himself is pulled down, so that
Estragon has to try to rescue him; but he too falls over, and all
four characters are now in a heap together with all the baggage.
At last, after much talk, Estragon and Vladimir get up of their
own accord, lift Pozzo to his feet, and prop him up between
them, for he is unable to stand alone. Estragon revenges himself
on the prostrate Lucky by kicking him savagely.

Pozzo, who lost his watch yesterday and so can no longer 'take
survey of all the world', has naturally also lost his memory, and
has deteriorated in physique as well as in his mind. When he
finally commands Lucky to get up and resume carrying the luggage, preparatory to starting off again, it appears that he has no
objective to reach but just goes aimlessly onward.

Vladimir would like Lucky to sing or dance or think once more
for their entertainment, but Pozzo says that he is now dumb.
'Since when?' asks the astonished Vladimir, wherat Pozzo becomes furious: 'Have you not done tormenting me with your

accursed time?' For him time has reached its stop, one day is identical with another, a lifetime has become an instant. With a striking image he summarizes his view of life:

'They give birth astride of a grave, the light gleams an instant, then it's night once more.' And on that he makes his exit, led by Lucky; but off the stage they fall down with a clatter, and presumably this marks their final disintegration.

Very shortly after their exit the boy messenger arrives, to repeat the same message as before, that Godot will not come today but will tomorrow without fail. While Estragon broods to one side Vladimir questions the boy about Mr Godot and learns that he does nothing. On being told that he has a beard Vladimir asks 'Fair or . . . (he hesitates) . . . or black?' The boy thinks that it is white, at which Vladimir exclaims 'Christ have mercy on us!' He was prepared to find that Godot was the Saviour or even the Devil; but appalled by the possibility of him being Jehovah, the God of the Judgement Day. He dismisses the boy, somewhat threateningly, with hesitant instructions to tell Mr Godot that he has seen him.

Estragon notices that Vladimir is visibly shaken by the boy's revelation, and they realize that it is now night and they must go. Estragon again suggests hanging, and they remove his belt and test its strength, but it breaks when they pull it. Estragon is in despair, and Vladimir promises that they shall hang themselves tomorrow, with a rope, unless Godot comes—but if he comes 'We'll be saved.' Finally they agree that they must go now, but they do not move, and the curtain falls.

There has been much debate as to the interpretation of Mr Godot. At first Vladimir seems to think of him as some sort of authoritative welfare officer who will explain their situation and suggest solutions; but later the implication of the white beard is that he is Lucky's God by whom some 'for reasons unknown but time will tell are plunged in torment plunged in fire.' In Act I Vladimir's attitude to Godot was 'I'm curious to hear what he has to offer. Then we'd take it or leave it.' But now, when Estragon asks, 'If we dropped him?' Vladimir replies 'He'd punish us.' However, I take Godot to be not Jehovah but another personification of the central self; a Mr Knott as dimly conceived by a Watt who is not yet ready to enter his house.

The interpretation of those fantastic characters Pozzo and Lucky is also debatable. Are they to be taken as two phases of a single person, like Moran and Molloy? And are Vladimir and

Estragon also two parts of the same person? It may well be so, especially when we notice how Estragon often approaches the inertia and stupor of Lucky, while Vladimir shows some affinities (his sense of time, his need for company, his concern about keeping an appointment) with the worldly Pozzo.

It is also possible that these four characters are Beckett's equivalent of William Blake's Four Zoas. Blake held that the perfect man maintained a harmonious balance between four functions of the psyche: Imagination, Reason, Passion, and bodily Sensation, which he personified as giants named Los, Urizen, Luvah and Tharmas. Man's Fall, and all evil, arose because these functions warred against each other; in particular Urizen tried to usurp power over the rest. In his Prophetic Books Blake gave various, and somewhat conflicting, accounts of this internal, psychological strife.

In Beckett's play it may well be that we have a different account of the same warfare within the split psyche. Pozzo corresponds to Tharmas, the sensations; he has enslaved Lucky, who corresponds to Urizen, or thought. The tender-hearted Vladimir is Luvah (feeling), and he alternately quarrels with and embraces the poet Estragon who represents imagination (Los). Whether these correspondences are accidental or intentional hardly matters; they are indubitably there and are just one more example of the extraordinary richness of meaning that is concealed inside this masterpiece.

## Breath

Beckett's 'dramaticule' *Breath*, (first performed at Oxford, 8th March, 1970) has neither actors nor words and lasts only thirty seconds. Against a scene of miscellaneous rubbish on the stage we hear the cry of a baby (taped) followed by a deep inhalation of breath while the lighting increases; then an exhalation with diminishing light and finally a repetition of the baby's cry.

The whole is a stage presentation of the summary of life given by Pozzo's exit line in Act 2—'They give birth astride of a grave, the light gleams an instant, then it's night once more.'

# Nine

# 'The Impossible Heap'

## Endgame

AFTER THE *Trilogy* and *Godot* were finished, six years went by before the next play, *Fin de Partie* (Endgame), was written; during this period Beckett was occupied with getting the French works published, with translating them himself into English, and also with writing the *Textes Pour Rien*. In this latter work he seems to be groping after a new statement of the old problems, but has not yet achieved the novel formulation of them which makes *How It Is* such an original work.

Endgame harks back rather to *Godot* than forward to the plays of the sixties. The four main characters of *Godot* are here condensed into two, Hamm and Clov. Hamm is in many ways a fusion of the tyrant Pozzo with the poet Estragon. Like Pozzo he is cruel, tyrannical, devoid of pity, and blind. He is a self-conscious actor, composing and declaiming a story with an artificial narrative voice and in Pozzo-like phraseology. However, he also has elements of Estragon, being imaginative and inward-looking, constantly wanting to sleep and dream romantic dreams. At one point he tells Clov 'I was never there . . . absent, always. It all happened without me. I don't know what's happened.' This is very like Estragon denying that he was ever in the Macon country with Vladimir and then adding 'It's possible. I didn't notice anything.' Neither Estragon nor Hamm are fully alive to the outer world.

In a similar way Clov combines the attributes of Lucky and Vladimir, at least in a large degree. Like Lucky he is a slave compelled (by his own nature) to obey a hated master whom he cannot leave. He has a 'stiff staggering' (i.e. catatonic) walk and is incapable of sitting down. However, he is far more rebellious and also more talkative than Lucky, and his speech is coherent and generally practical though his actions with the ladder and telescope

H

when he wants to look out of the windows show some mental confusion.

Clov resembles Vladimir chiefly in the fact that he is the one who is aware of external reality and deals with the practical matters. He reports to Hamm on the deserted land and sea outside the house; he looks after his master, feeds him, manages the kitchen, and fetches whatever is demanded. So too Vladimir was the one who noticed external things—the sore on Lucky's neck, Lucky's hat on the ground, Estragon's abandoned boots, and the new leaves on the tree. It was Vladimir who provided the carrots or turnips that Estragon ate and was concerned about finding shelter for the night.

The mutual dependence of the two couples in *Godot* is, naturally, carried on here between Hamm and Clov. Though the latter says 'If I could kill him I'd die happy', and often declares that he will leave, he knows very well that he cannot do so. Hamm, unable to get up from his chair, is utterly dependent on Clov, but the latter is equally dependent on Hamm.

HAMM:          Gone from me you'd be dead.
CLOV:          And vice versa.

As two halves of one split self they cannot be separated. This is why at the end of the play, in spite of Clov's bag, umbrella and overcoat, suggesting his immediate departure, he does not in fact actually go.

The stage setting, a bare room with two windows, like eyes, and the lighting grey (the colour of brain matter), seems to symbolize the inside of a skull, one of Beckett's favourite images. In the centre of the stage, in an armchair on castors, Hamm is asleep under an old sheet. His position, and later on his insistence on being put back in the precise centre, symbolizes his role as the inner self. His counterpart, Clov, the false self, is standing by the door watching him. After a few moments Clov draws back the curtains and looks out of the windows. Then he peers into two dustbins which stand on one side of the stage, and finally goes to Hamm and removes the covering sheet. The sleeping figure is revealed as an old man in a dressing gown with a blood-stained handkerchief over his face.

While Hamm still sleeps Clov speaks the opening words which state the main theme of the play, the paradox of the necessity for, and the impossibility of, time stopping: 'Finished, it's finished, nearly finished, it must be nearly finished. (Pause) Grain upon grain, one by one, and one day, suddenly, there's a heap, a little heap, the impossible heap.' The echo of the last words on the Cross evokes the image of Zeno's heap, with the millet grains transformed into moments of time. Later, Hamm uses the same metaphor: 'Moment upon moment, pattering down, like the millet grains of . . . (he hesitates) . . . that old Greek, and all life long you wait for that to mount up to a life.'

After Clov has gone out Hamm wakes up and removes the handkerchief from his face, revealing that he wears black glasses, for he is blind. Yawning, he says 'Me—to play', and goes through some meticulous motions of wiping the glasses, folding his handkerchief neatly, clearing his throat, and joining the tips of his fingers—all of which emphasize his resemblance to Pozzo. He begins his speech with an echo from *The Lamentations*: 'Can there be misery—(he yawns)—loftier than mine?' And having considered this question dispassionately he too adverts to the main theme: 'Yes, there it is, it's time it ended and yet I hesitate to— (he yawns)—to end.'

The two men differ somewhat in their appreciation of time. To the outward-looking false self, Clov, time is still very real; yesterday means something definite to him; he longs for an end but he is not very close to it. For Hamm, on the other hand, time means very little; he attaches no meaning to yesterday. When he asks Clov what time it is, the reply—'The same as usual'—suggests that time is not flowing on; for Hamm, partly because of his age and partly because of his blindness, time has nearly stopped. And if time, 'which takes survey of all the world,' has slowed down almost to stopping point, so also the external world, viewed by Clov through the windows, has become dead, featureless and empty. Hamm comments that nature has forgotten them, to which Clov replies: 'There's no more nature.' But Hamm thinks that is an exaggeration, for they still breathe and slowly decay; time and nature do still continue to function, though minimally. Things too have disappeared from the world to a surprising extent; in the course of the play we learn that there are no more bicycle wheels, sugarplums, rugs or pain-killer, though there is one flea and a dying rat. The economy of Hamm's household is running down and cannot be replenished from the dead world without.

Soon we discover that the two dustbins on the stage contain Hamm's senile parents, Nagg and Nell. Like Mahood in his jar, they are legless trunks, treated as rubbish by their pitiless son; a picture of 'unregarded age in corners thrown' that perhaps only Swift could have equalled. When Nagg pushes the lid up and demands his pap he is greeted as 'accursed progenitor', given a biscuit, and bottled up again.

When he appears again he knocks on the next bin to waken Nell, and they converse a little, reminiscing about the time when they lost their legs through a crash on their tandem while cycling in France, and their holiday on Lake Como when they became engaged. Meanwhile Hamm has been trying to dream about happier days when he made love in the woods, and his parents' chatter annoys him; finally Nagg's persistence in recounting a funny story puts Hamm in a rage and he tells Clov to chuck the bins into the sea. However, Clov merely pushes the old couple down and shuts the lids after first ascertaining that Nell has no pulse. As she does not appear again we may assume that she is now dead, and indeed, later, Clov looks into her bin and reports that she looks as if she were dead.

Nagg, however, remains alive, for a little later he reappears and makes a significant revelation. We learn from him that as a small boy Hamm doted on his father, not his mother. 'Whom did you call when you were a tiny boy, and were frightened, in the dark? Your mother? No. Me.' And this is immediately followed by two lines which reveal the callous egotism which must have turned the boy's love to hatred: 'And we let you cry. Then we moved you out of earshot, so that we might sleep in peace.'

These lines expose a situation which is typical for the genesis of a schizoidal development in a child—the betrayal of his trust in his parents and an undermining of his sense of security. After this one can realize that the dustbins were inevitable.

The relationship of Clov to Hamm, who is his father (whether natural or by adoption is not clear), parallels in some degree that of Hamm to Nagg. There is the same hatred in both, together with the necessity for the son to look after the father in his old age —for without this inner compulsion neither son would have tolerated his father's presence. Naturally the parents are not grateful for their sons' attentions, although Hamm does get so far as a formal, polite thanks near the end: 'I'm obliged to you, Clov. For your services.' But Nagg's last words are bitter: 'Yes, I hope I'll live till then, to hear you calling me like when you were a tiny boy, and were frightened, in the dark, and I was your only hope.'

After this repetition of paternal callousness Nagg knocks in vain on Nell's dustbin and getting no reply sinks back into his own and closes the lid. When, a little later, Clov lifts the lid to see if he is still alive, he is found to be crying; and Hamm remarks 'Then he's living.' This harks back to the comment when Vladimir said that the willow tree must be dead, whereupon Estragon added 'No more weeping.' After this no more is heard of Nagg or Nell and both may be presumed dead, or perhaps not.

Having disposed of his parents for the time being, Hamm makes Clov wheel him round the room, hugging the wall beyond which is what he calls 'the other hell', the world of his own mind being the first hell. But he tires of this half-hearted approach towards an external world before completing the circuit, and makes Clov wheel him back and place him precisely at the centre, a point about which he fusses like an old woman, for only when 'bang in the centre' does he feel safe.

This accomplished, he makes Clov fetch ladder and telescope to report on the state of the external world as seen from the two windows. On land and sea all is empty, there is no sun and the light is grey. To his query of what is happening Clov can only answer that 'something is taking its course', which leads Hamm to consider as a very faint possibility that perhaps their lives might after all have some meaning.

Clov now is bitten by a flea, which provokes Hamm to cry out: 'But humanity might start from there all over again! Catch him, for the love of God!' So Clov fetches the insecticide and averts this danger. Soon afterwards Hamm, mindful that Clov should survive him and thus decay alone in an empty world, prophesies: 'One day you'll be blind like me. You'll be sitting there, a speck in the void, in the dark, for ever, like me.' And he elaborates a picture of Clov alone, blind, helpless in an empty world, like Hamm in all things except for the fact that he won't have any companion because he has never had pity on anyone—and also because there is no one left. But has Hamm ever had pity on anyone? Two stories, of Mother Pegg and of the man with a boy, seem to deny it.

It appears that Mother Pegg was an old woman whom Hamm now remembers as having been bonny once 'like a flower of the field. And a great one for the men.' But when in her old age she begged for some oil for her lamp Hamm turned her away and she died, as Clov declares, of darkness. Hamm tries feebly to excuse himself on the ground that he hadn't any oil, but Clov insists that he had.

The second story is one that Hamm appears to be composing

as he goes along. He tells it to Nagg and Clov in a theatrical narrator's voice with little digressions of self-approval and artificial attempts at verisimilitude—'Zero by the thermometer,' 'fifty by the heliometer,' 'a hundred by the anemometer.' But the tale itself may be a sadistic phantasy or an actual reminiscence; in either case it reveals his pitiless nature.

One Christmas eve, he says, a man came crawling on his belly towards him, begging for bread to take back to his son whom he had left three days ago alone at home. Hamm received him coldly, declaring that he had no bread. When asked for some corn he agreed that he had some of that, but suppose he were to give him enough to make a pot of porridge for the boy, assuming the child was still alive when his father returned, what good would that do?

'I lost patience. (violently) Use your head, can't you, use your head, you're on earth, there's no cure for that.' Then, calming down, he offered to take the man into his service, but the fellow asked if he would take the child as well.

'It was the moment I was waiting for. (Pause) Would I consent to take in the child. . . . (Pause) I can see him still, down on his knees, his hands flat on the ground, glaring at me with his mad eyes, in defiance of my wishes.' Clearly it was not the man but Hamm who was glaring with mad eyes, for this story, whether it is pure phantasy or based on memory, is the work of a maniac.

After some desultory conversation Clov starts tidying up. He likes order.

'It's my dream. A world where all would be silent and still and each thing in its last place, under the last dust.' Not, be it noticed, the order of things put neatly in their right places for convenience in future use, but the order of final disposition in death. However, Hamm will not let him tidy up; he wants to continue his ghastly story and Clov also wants to hear how it ends. But Hamm feels 'rather drained' by what he calls the 'prolonged creative effort'; actually, of course, it is the manic fit which has exhausted him. Now that he is calmer he wants to be wheeled under the window so that he may feel the light on his face and hear the sea.

When he returns to his central place he gives vent to a series of disjointed remarks, some expressing remorse, some hatred, and some his wish for death. 'All those I might have helped. (Pause) Helped! (Pause) Saved! (Pause) Saved! (Pause) The place was crawling with them!'

'When it wasn't bread they wanted it was crumpets. (Pause. violently) Out of my sight and back to your petting parties.'

'All kinds of fantasies! That I'm being watched! A rat! Steps!
Breath held and then . . . then babble, babble words—'
And he ends this speech (which is a good example of the disordered thought of a schizophrenic) with the metaphor of the
millet grains which I have already quoted: 'And all life long you
wait for that to mount up to a life.'

It is now time for Hamm to be given his pain-killer, but alas!
the box is empty and there is no more. Hamm is naturally appalled
for the moment, but he soon calms down and makes Clov go to
the windows and tell him what the earth and the sea are like now.
Clov, who has been getting out of patience declares that this is the
last time he will look out. He takes the telescope and is reporting
with satisfaction that there is nothing to be seen, when suddenly
he spies a small boy. Here the French version differs from the
English one. The English account is much shorter. Clov wants to
take the gaff and kill the boy, 'a potential procreator', but Hamm
restrains him. In the French version (which is the original one)
Hamm orders Clov to go and exterminate the boy. Moreover he
evokes the image of Jesus, of Moses, and (since the boy appears
to be contemplating his navel) of Buddha. In both versions the
implication is that, like the leaves on the dead tree, the boy is a
symbol of hope, of rebirth; and it leads Hamm to utter his own
sort of *Nunc Dimittis*: 'It's the end, Clov, we've come to the end.
I don't need you any more.'

Clov says he will leave Hamm, whereupon Hamm begs him to
say a few parting words which he can treasure up; but Clov cannot
rise to a sentimental farewell, and only launches out into a pessimistic speech ending 'when I fall I'll weep for happiness.' He goes
towards the door while Hamm self-consciously, like the actor he
is, settles himself down to compose a speech for his death scene.
We have been prepared for the theatricality of the final scene by a
number of examples of stage jargon which Hamm has used
already—his reference to an aside, a soliloquy, an underplot, etc.
Professor Kenner has made much of all this, as also of the chess
metaphors contained in the play, but I think he has missed the
main point. Hamm (like Pozzo) is not a complete person; he is
to that extent unreal and he tries by dramatizing himself to
achieve a sense of personal identity. Of all professions the actor's
is the most schizoidal, for he must allow at least a portion of his
psyche to identify with the part that he is playing. Conversely, the
schizoid is compelled to create a spurious self, to act a part, in his
effort to become a person.

During the closing speech Clov retires to the kitchen but soon reappears dressed for departure, with hat, coat, umbrella and bag. He stands by the door silently watching his master to the end.

Hamm meanwhile throws down the gaff, raises and replaces his skull-cap, wipes his glasses, all very meticulously, making little comments on his actions. Then he composes a line of poetry: 'You cried for night; it falls: now cry in darkness.' Although this is one of the bitterest lines ever written, his only comment is one of self-satisfaction: 'Nicely put, that.' He follows it with a statement of the unreality of time. 'Moments for nothing, now as always, time was never and time is over.' Then he reverts to his cruel story of the man to whom he refused bread, and having now touched on three important themes—the misery of life, the illusion of time, and the cruelty of man—he resigns himself to his end.

Having whistled to see if Clov is still there, and called out to his father, with no reply from either, he throws the whistle away, drops the toy dog which Clov had made for him, and calls once more, softly, to Clov who remains silent. Accepting that he is now left alone to die he composes himself in the chair and covers his face with the handkerchief. With Clov standing motionless by the door watching him the scene is just as it was at the start of the play, except for the fact that Clov is now dressed for departure and Hamm is not covered by the sheet. We are left to assume that Hamm and his parents are now dead and that Clov will wander out into an unreal world.

Unlike the novels, which are based on the quest for the 'glassy essence' of man, these two plays, *Godot* and *Endgame*, are more concerned with existence; and this will also be a feature of the next three plays. Estragon and Vladimir, Hamm and Clov, represent the inner and the false selves of a split personality; but they are not so divorced from reality or so disintegrated as Watt or Malone. True, they are presented in a phantastic setting, but they constitute a commentary on real life. And this is still more the case in the next few plays whose characters, though still of schizoidal type, are living in an everyday world and, although on the verge of senility, are not manifestly psychotic.

# Act Without Words I

*Endgame* is followed by a short mime for one actor who is confronted with various tantalizing situations symbolizing the arbitrary and irrational nature of man's experience in this life. First the man is flung violently from the wings on to an empty stage, a desert under a dazzling light. This entry illustrates Beckett's favourite view of birth as being a forcible ejection of the child who wishes to remain in the womb; and the man on the stage twice tries to return to the wings but is again flung back to face life willy-nilly.

Now there descends from the flies first a tree, whose shade-giving tuft of leaves closes up directly he sits down under it; then a pair of tailor's scissors and a tiny carafe of water which remains just above his reach. After this, three cubes of different sizes appear, but when he stands on them to reach the water the carafe is raised so that he cannot grasp it.

After this a rope descends, but as he climbs it this too is drawn up, so that he has to cut it in order to fall back on the ground. Having now a length of rope he wishes to hang himself on the bough of the tree, but is once more foiled as the bough immediately folds itself down against the trunk. He next turns to the scissors, hoping to cut his throat, but they, together with the cubes, disappear up into the flies.

Now he gives up the struggle and lies down motionless on the ground, nor can he be tempted even when the carafe of water is lowered close to his face. Finally both carafe and tree are pulled up, and the man remains, defeated, having opted out of the struggle, lying on the empty desert.

The mime, with a first-class actor, can be a fine piece of comic clowning; it can also be taken as a parody of those experiments that psychologists make when they try to investigate the intelligence of apes and other animals, whose feelings may well be those of the man in the mime. But the significance of the act is that it symbolizes in concrete visible terms Gloucester's despairing cry: 'As flies to wanton boys are we to the Gods.' Here, however, the man is not killed but mocked and tormented for their sport. He is not even allowed to commit suicide, so he can only fall into protective apathy and cease to pay any attention to the futile world of phenomena. His final gesture is to look at his hands, those tools which at first seemed to promise so much but in the event have proved useless.

# *Ten*

# 'All That Old Misery'

## All That Fall

Among BECKETT'S PLAYS *All That Fall*, though written for radio, most nearly approaches what the average theatre-goer expects to see on the stage. It is not set in some symbolic limbo but in the Irish countryside, on a road and at a railway station. The characters are ordinary people living and moving in the commonsense world and they are concerned with everyday matters. Being a radio play it substitutes aural for visual perception, so that we hear the appropriate noises instead of seeing the action, and sometimes the effect is ludicrous—after all it is not necessary whenever an animal is mentioned for us to hear it bleat or moo or chirp. But why then did the author insert six of these childish noises in one of Mrs Rooney's speeches in which she is actually commenting on the silence and emptiness of the countryside? Surely only to puncture the sentimental poetic vein into which she has dropped. For the main theme of the play, namely the inevitable misery of old age and death, is ironically interwoven with typically Irish comedy, which actually intensifies the tragedy.

At the opening, while Mrs Rooney is dragging herself painfully along the road to the station to meet Dan, her blind husband, we hear strains of *Death and the Maiden*, and the same tune is heard again just before the end of the play when she is returning. The references to death and severe illness are numerous; five of the characters to whom Mrs Rooney talks, though healthy themselves, have a wife, daughter or father severely ill; a hen is killed on the road, and Mrs Rooney mourns for her daughter Minnie who died while still a child.

Mrs Rooney in her seventies is fat and ailing and knows she is decaying; but she still takes some interest in other people, enquires after their dependants, and still appreciates the beauty of the laburnum and of the lambs. She has been educated, and tends to talk in an artificial literary style:

'Let us halt a moment, and let this vile dust fall back upon the viler worms.'

The comic passages of her conversation with Mr Tyler and Mr Slocum on the road are interspersed with moments of misery and self-pity.

'Oh I am just a hysterical old hag I know, destroyed with sorrow and pining and gentility and church-going and fat and rheumatism and childlessness.' And a little later she sobs with grief for the loss of her daughter Minnie who would by now be a woman of fifty had she lived.

When she at last arrives at the station she is offended by the fact that Miss Fitt, a fellow communicant at church, does not recognize her. Miss Fitt is a religious type of schizoid, who prides herself on being 'very distray' and justifies her non-recognition by claiming that in church she is 'alone with my Maker' so that she never sees people there, nor even the collection plate when it comes round. She did not deliberately cut Mrs Rooney, for 'All I saw was a big pale blur.' But all this comedy is annulled by Mrs Rooney's rueful comment: 'Maddy Rooney, née Dunne, the big pale blur. (Pause) You have piercing sight, Miss Fitt, if you only knew it, literally piercing.' Underneath the superficial recognizable personality of Mrs Rooney there should be an autonomous self, an identity, but in her case this is indefinite, formless, and uncertain—a pale blur.

At the station everyone is waiting for the train which most unaccountably is now a quarter of an hour late. There is speculation as to the reason, and some anxiety. When at last it arrives Mr Rooney, the old blind man, is not seen at first and Maddy has a moment of despair, but then her Dan appears leaning on Jerry, the boy who earns a penny by meeting him. Today, however, is Dan's birthday, though he has forgotten it, and so Maddy has toiled up to greet him.

Dan is almost senile and has many schizoidal traits in common with the M's of the novels. He is 'near' with money, like Moran; loves calculation, like Murphy or Molloy; has moments of blankness and mental absence; easily loses the thread of his discourse; hankers after solitude and inertness; is liable to sudden changes of mood, and carries in his pocket an enigmatic object which looks like, but is not, a kind of ball.

Dan and Maddy start their journey home from the station with Dan calculating how much a cab would have cost, then complaining that the number of steps down from the platform is always varying—a Watt-like trait! When Maddy asks him the cause of the train's delay he murmurs 'Good God' quietly, and when she pursues the matter he loses his temper. She insists further, but he asserts that he knows nothing. Shortly after this, when some children jeer at them, he asks Maddy if she had ever wished to kill a child, and admits that he has often nearly attacked the boy Jerry. He then switches the conversation to his own ailments, but soon begins a detached narration of the journey.

He says he was alone in his compartment, 'at least I hope so, for I made no attempt to restrain myself,' and was occupied in calculating all the expenses involved in his travelling and office attendance, concluding that if only he stayed at home in bed the gain would be considerable. On the other hand, the horrors of home-life with all its attendant household chores, day in and day out, would be insupportable. So he prefers to go to his silent city office, 'to be buried there alive, if only from ten to five,' in the same spirit as Murphy envying the luxury of the padded cell. Suddenly he noticed that the train had stopped, and though at first he was unperturbed he soon became uneasy and paced up and down the compartment. After a long while the train moved off and he got off at the station. That is all he can say about the journey.

Maddy says nothing to all this, and Dan evidently fears that she doesn't believe him. She talks, apparently irrelevantly, about a former visit to a mind specialist who told her of a little girl whom he had failed to cure and who had died; and he had made the strange statement: 'The trouble with her was she had never been really born!' In other words this girl had never achieved a sense of her own individuality, her personal identity. The psychiatrist's words have haunted Mrs Rooney, presumably because she vaguely felt that, like 'the big pale blur', they applied to herself.

Maddy's thoughts pursue strange byways. She asserts that Jesus rode on a hinny, not an ass's colt; and the sparrows of the text, 'than many of which we are of more value', weren't sparrows at all. To which the dour Dan asks: 'Does that put our price up?'

When they come near the house, in which the record of *Death and the Maiden* is still playing, Dan murmurs the title indistinctly and starts crying silently. Then he asks Maddy what the text for tomorrow's sermon is and learns that it is: 'The Lord upholdeth all that fall and raiseth all those that be bowed down.' The irony of this, after all the misery, illness and death which they have suffered or encountered in others, makes them burst into wild laughter.

At this point Jerry comes running after them to give Dan the curious ball-like object which he had dropped on the platform. Dan will not explain it to the inquisitive Maddy, but just says it is a thing he carries about with him. Maddy asks Jerry if he knows what caused the train to be so late, but Dan immediately says the boy couldn't possibly know. As Maddy persists he tells her to leave the boy alone and come home. Quite obviously he is anxious to prevent Maddy hearing the cause, but he fails, for Jerry blurts out that a little child had fallen out of the carriage: 'On to the line, Ma'am. (Pause) Under the wheels, Ma'am.' And at this Dan groans.

Here the play ends, and their footsteps die away as Dan and Maddy go silently along the road. It is possibly the most moving play that Beckett has written.

There are numerous little pointers leading us to suspect that Dan had pushed the child out of his carriage in a moment of mania. He has a schizoidal mentality and whenever the delay is mentioned his reaction is peculiar and he shows emotional disturbance; and he had admitted to Maddy that he had been tempted to attack Jerry. But this is not a police drama, and the important thing is not whether the child fell accidentally or was pushed out by a maniac; the crux is that in either case the child's death was an arbitrary, irrational happening. It is what Joyce would have called an 'epiphany', revealing the intrinsically irrational nature of the universe.

# Krapp's Last Tape

This short playlet, written in 1958, is a moving study of a disillusioned old man looking back on a life of failure. His negligent dress, the dirty white shirt with no collar, the dirty white boots, the unshaven face all show that he has ceased to bother about appearances, and his purple nose reveals the tippler.

Krapp sits at a table on which are a tape-recorder and some boxes containing (as we are told) recorded tapes. A few minutes are spent while he examines a key, walks round the table and unlocks a drawer, extracts a banana from it, eats it meditatively, gets out a second banana which he starts to bite but finally puts in his pocket, then goes to the back of the stage and has a drink, before finally coming back to the table bringing with him a ledger in which details of the various tapes are written.

He hunts for Box Three, Spool Five (words which he repeats with evident relish as if gloating over an anticipated treat), and reads out from the ledger a summary of its contents. These include 'Slight improvement of bowel condition,' 'Memorable equinox' and 'Farewell to love.'

During this search for the required spool we learn casually that there are nine boxes, and we may assume that each contains five spools (the last box is full of used tapes because later, when he wants to speak into a virgin tape, he has to get it from the drawer); thus there are forty-five used tapes altogether. As spool five of box three is the fifteenth, and we soon learn that it was recorded on his thirty-ninth birthday, we may calculate that he is now seventy years old, and also that he began this series of birthday recordings on his twenty-fifth birthday. This last fact explains why Beckett, writing in 1958, should have taken the trouble to set the play in the future; for of course a septuagenarian in 1958 could not have begun his tape-recording in 1913. It is no doubt a very minor point, but indicative of Beckett's meticulous attention to details.

Krapp switches on this tape and listens to the comments of his thirty-nine-year-old self on the past year. He was evidently at that time an introspective solitary man, serious minded, concerned with his bodily health and intellectual powers. Like Murphy he was absorbed in himself.

'The new light above my table is a great improvement. With all this darkness round me I feel less alone. (Pause) In a way. (Pause) I love to get up and move about in it, then back here to . . . (hesitates) . . . me. (Pause) Krapp.' And we note that Krapp himself is sitting under a strong light above the table and is surrounded by a stage in darkness.

Soon the tape voice says that he has just been listening to a previous birthday recording of some ten or twelve years back. The tape-voice is scornful about 'that young whelp' and laughs sardonically at his aspirations and good resolutions about cutting down on drink and sex. We also gather that the younger man was living 'off and on' with a girl, but all that the thirty-nine-year-old Krapp can say about her is that her eyes were incomparable but that he is well out of that 'hopeless business'. Evidently his twenty-eighth (?) year now appears to him to have been barren, for he concludes by asking 'what remains of all that misery?'

At this point Krapp switches off and retires for another two or three drinks, sings a snatch of *Now the day is over* and comes back to resume his listening. The voice refers to his mother's death in the autumn and his vigil outside in the cold while he waited and wished for her demise. We hear that the past year was one of profound spiritual gloom until on a stormy night in March (the 'memorable equinox') he experienced a psychological 'conversion', a re-orientation of his whole attitude to life similar in form, though apparently not in content, to a religious or mystical ecstasy.

'I suddenly saw the whole thing. The vision at last . . . what I suddenly saw then was this, that the belief I had been going on all my life, namely—', but at this point Krapp switches off impatiently, so that we never learn the nature and content of this vision, nor what his new belief was. Krapp is not interested in his former ideals, which he has evidently discarded as fallacies. He winds the tape forward to reach the bit for which he chose this particular tape; it depicts him making love to a girl in a punt which drifted down the stream and stuck among the irises.

'I lay down across her with my face in her breasts and my hand on her. We lay there without moving. But under us all moved, and moved us, gently, up and down, and from side to side.' Here Krapp switches off, broods awhile, goes backstage for another drink, returns and unlocks a drawer, and takes out an unused tape which he puts on the machine in place of spool five. He starts (characteristically forgetting to switch on first) to record his summary of his sixty-ninth year, beginning with a sneer at 'that stupid bastard I took myself for thirty years ago,' and then brooding on the eyes of that girl in the punt, eyes which held all the joy and sorrow of life within them. But the younger Krapp had said farewell to love lest it should 'take his mind off his homework', i.e. the pursuit of his new vision. This was indicated in the early part of the love scene: 'I said again I thought it was hopeless and no good going on and she agreed.' At thirty-nine Krapp could not let his 'me' be invaded or subordinated by another self.

Krapp can recall nothing significant to record about the past year; he has only sat outside in the park once or twice in the summer, sold seventeen copies of his book, and shed bitter tears reading *Effie*—which seems to be not only the title of a book (his own?) but also the name of the girl with whom he could have been happy.

The year has been an empty one. 'What's a year now? The sour cud and the iron stool'; a judgement which reminds one of Malone's summary of life: 'Dish and pot, these are the poles.'

Krapp considers abandoning the recording, and going to bed
to lie awake and recall to mind the few tolerably happy moments
of his early life, to gather again the holly at Christmas or listen
again to the church bells on a Sunday. But he comments sardonically: 'Be again, be again. (Pause) All that old misery. (Pause)
Once wasn't enough for you.' And after another pause his mind
reverts to the punt and he says 'Lie down across her.'

Suddenly he tears the tape off, throws it away, and puts spool
five on again, winding it forward to the vital passage. He listens
once more to the love scene which was the only experience of self-
validating existence in his life, but which he had rejected from a
fear that his ego would be swamped; instead, he had tried to follow a vision which was delusive and hollow, the product of a
false conception of the self. This rejection of a genuine relationship with another, for the sake of preserving an isolated narrow
'me', is the whole tragedy of the play.

While Krapp broods over the past the tape runs on to the final
words: 'Perhaps my best years are gone. When there was a chance
of happiness. But I wouldn't want them back. Not with the fire
in me now. No, I wouldn't want them back.'

But alas, at seventy Krapp does want just this one portion back.

Krapp indeed is Beckett's Peer Gynt. His birthday tapes
enshrine a series of discarded false selves, like the layers which
Peer stripped off the onion in the vain hope of finding the central
kernel. But Beckett does not allow the Solveig whom Krapp
rejected to be found waiting faithfully for him in old age. Krapp
will die as he has lived, alone.

# Embers

This radio playlet appears in the same volume as *Krapp's Last
Tape* and, like it, consists of a monologue by a lonely old man who
is talking to himself, to his dead father, and also conversing with
the hallucinatory voice of his dead wife.

Sitting on the seashore Henry talks to himself ostensibly to
drown the sound of the waves which both frightens and yet
fascinates him. He cannot keep away from the sea which drowned
his father who had despised the boy Henry as a weakling and a
wash-out. We find that Henry in his turn dislikes his own
daughter, Addie. 'Horrid little child, wish we'd never had her.'
We hear sounds of this girl having her piano lesson and also a

riding lesson, two accomplishments forced on her by her mother, and both lessons end in wailing.

The relation of Henry to his wife, Ada, was not much better than to his father or his daughter. He found her conversation intolerable: 'that's what hell will be like, small chat to the babbling of Lethe about the good old days when we wished we were dead. (Pause) Price of margarine fifty years ago. (Pause) And now.' Nevertheless he wants her company now, and when he invokes her the dead Ada's voice answers. She is disturbed at his habit of talking to himself, and urges him to consult his doctor, Holloway.

Now before his comments on his daughter and his evocation of Ada's voice Henry had begun to tell himself a story about two old men, Bolton and Holloway. Bolton has called in the doctor at midnight because he is in 'great trouble'. It is a bitter winter's night, and he is alone in the dark, standing by the dying fire. The doctor is irritated at having to come out to what is clearly a psychological not a physical 'case'.

After his conversation with Ada, Henry resumes this story. Holloway offers to give Bolton an injection, but Bolton merely plays with the curtains; then he lights a candle and looks Holloway in the face. Holloway wants to get away. 'We've had this before, Bolton, don't ask me to go through it again,' he says. And Bolton can only implore him, 'Please, Please!' What exactly he demands of the doctor is not explained, and the significance of the scene, apart from the inability of the one to communicate his mental trouble to the other, is obscure. However, I think we may accept that Bolton stands for Henry himself and that the doctor, Holloway, is being identified with his father, with Ada, and also with Christ—in fact he represents all the potential sources of strength and comfort to whom Henry had turned in vain for understanding and support. Holloway is the final surrogate for these, and he too fails.

Consider these lines on the final page: 'that was always it, night, and the embers cold, and the glim shaking in your old fist, saying Please! Please! (Pause) Begging— (Pause) of the poor. (Pause) Ada! (Pause) Father! (Pause) Christ!'

Why does Beckett suddenly use the second-person 'your' in a story where before and after this he uses 'his'? Surely it is an intentional slip indicating that Henry has for the moment forgotten to maintain the fiction of Bolton and thus reveals that he is really telling himself a story about himself, a fictional situation symbolizing his own real isolation.

I

On the whole, in spite of the emotional force of many of the lines, I feel this playlet contains too many obscurities to be wholly successful. One asks, for instance, what is the significance of the sound of hooves which is mentioned three times apart from their appropriate appearance during Addie's riding lesson. Is Addie dead too? And if so, was she killed while riding? And what occurred on the mysterious occasion when Henry could not be found and his father went out and sat on a rock and looked out to sea? Was it then that he was drowned? These are some of the uncertainties which to me detract from the play, though perhaps Beckett deliberately contrived them because life is largely made up of obscure and seemingly unrelated situations.

# Eh Joe

In 1966 B.B.C Television produced a short playlet, *Eh Joe*, which belongs rather to the plays in this chapter, in which the stress is on human suffering, than to the more abstract ones written in the sixties. It is a mime for a silent actor who listens to the inner voice which he cannot silence and which reproaches him, recalling the past that he has tried to push out of his mind.

First we see Joe, a dishevelled ageing man, alone in his bedroom closing the window, drawing the curtain, locking all doors and peering under the bed to ensure that there is no witness to his existence; and then he sits on the bed, closes his eyes and waits for oblivion.

A quiet, distinct woman's voice calling his name makes him open his eyes. She begins by ironically suggesting that he switch off the light lest perhaps a louse may be watching him. Then she reminds him that when his father died Joe kept on hearing the dead man's voice, and again after his mother's death he heard her's, and so it was also with others who had loved him. He had been loved by many; but in each case he had succeeded in silencing these voices by a process of 'mental thuggee', and now there is no one alive who loves him. The present voice is that of a woman who once had loved him too, but she had fortunately escaped in time and found a better love; for though Joe was loved by others he never could give back love in return. He fled (like the young Krapp) from any deep entanglement which threatened to enchain his precious ego.

The voice reminds him that although she herself broke away

successfully there was another girl whose rejection by Joe led
her to suicide. Like Goethe's Harper she had eaten her bread
with tears and endured nights of weeping. ('Ah, she knew you,
heavenly powers') before despair drove her to the seashore. Twice
she failed in her attempt, but the third time she swallowed a tube
of tablets and lay down with her face on the pebbles calling Joe's
name to the stones until the incoming tide silenced her.

'There's love for you . . . wouldn't you say? . . . compared to us
. . . compared to Him. . . . Eh Joe?'

# *Eleven*

# 'Moments For Nothing'

## Happy Days

IN EACH NEW WORK Beckett demands of the reader or spectator that he should abandon some hitherto cherished convention and accept some new and apparently outrageous literary or theatrical technique or some impossible symbolical unreality. In this play we are offered a stream-of-consciousness monologue delivered by a middle-aged woman who is buried up to her waist (and in Act 2 up to her neck) in a mound of earth in the middle of an empty sun-scorched plain. Behind the mound, and for the most part out of sight, her sixty-year-old husband dwells in a hole, reads his newspaper, and occasionally says a few words. There is no build-up of a dramatic situation, no conflict of characters, no significant action, no denouement—nothing that a playgoer normally expects from a drama on the stage. We are just presented with a given symbolical situation which remains to the end substantially what it was at the beginning.

When the curtain rises Winnie is revealed asleep in her mound, but she is awakened by the clang of a bell and her day begins with a short prayer. This done she turns to the real business of the day, which is to produce the illusion of happiness by killing time until the bell shall ring again to tell her the day is over and she can sleep.

'Ah yes, so little to say, so little to do, and the fear so great, certain days, of finding oneself . . . left, with hours still to run, before the bell for sleep.'

Whether this picture of the unreality of a life consisting of futile actions undertaken merely to kill time is meant specifically for Winnie or generally for all mankind is left an open question. Beckett never preaches a doctrine or offers a solution or a philosophical formula.

And how does Winnie kill time? Mainly by talking to herself and at intervals to Willie, who seldom replies, and by occupying herself with trivial actions with the various objects contained in a shopping bag that providentially lies beside her on the mound. Like Malone she has her quota of possessions, but whereas his held significant, even if repressed, memories of his past history, hers are merely useful adjuncts (mostly toiletries which minister to her vanity) which enable her to create the illusion of living.

These objects also have a technical value, for the stage 'business' which the actress extracts from the toothbrush, spectacles, mirror, lipstick, nail-file, etc., etc., enables her to keep the audience's attention and to achieve the seemingly impossible feat of making a flow of banalities interesting and significant. Not that the actress is allowed free play with these things; Beckett has written meticulous directions for almost every phrase, such as (puts on spectacles), (closes eyes), (long pause), (smile off) and so on—in fact there must be nearly as many words of stage directions as are spoken in the play.

Besides the toiletries already mentioned, the bag contains other things, and notably a revolver, which may suggest that in her weaker moments Winnie could contemplate suicide, for on first taking it out she kisses it before putting it back again. Later, however, she is annoyed when she pulls it out unintentionally and she asks Willie if he remembers that he used to beg her to take it from him lest he should do away with himself—so we assume that Willie has suicidal tendencies. She then apostrophizes the revolver:

'Oh I suppose it's a comfort to know you are there, but I'm tired of you. (Pause) I'll leave you out, that's what I'll do (she lays the revolver on ground to her right).' And so the revolver stays on view, never touched but yet conveniently to hand, a potential way-out for her or for Willie. It's importance is shown by the stage direction for Act 2, which specifically mentions that it is 'conspicuous to her right on mound.'

Winnie is a pseudo-personality whose second-hand life consists of convention and sentimentality, as her speech does of clichés. She has never achieved a genuine relationship with anyone, not excepting her husband, and she must constantly bolster herself up with the delusion that she is happy and that there is 'so much to be thankful for, great mercies.' She reminds one of those 'last men' of Nietzsche's, who say that they have discovered happiness, and blink. Her assertions of happiness are apt to ring hollow and trail out in uncertainty.

'What a happy day for me . . . it will have been. (Pause) So far.' Having said her ritual morning prayer Winnie brushes her teeth and becomes engrossed in trying to decipher the inscription on the brush handle. The words 'fully guaranteed genuine pure hog's setae' lead her to reflect how wonderful it is that every day brings some little addition to one's knowledge if only one takes pains with it. And if one cannot take the pains, why then one must just close the eyes and wait for the happy day of release from consciousness—'That is what I find so comforting when I lose heart and envy the brute beast.' This theme of the intolerable burden of consciousness, here incidentally adumbrated, will be expanded in the next drama, *Play*; but in this one Winnie is convincing herself that life is really good: 'Not a day goes by—(Smile)—to speak in the old style—(Smile off)—without some blessing—in disguise.' And her day is spent, with the help of numerous trivial actions with lipstick, nail-file, etc., etc., in a stream of disjointed reflections on life, fragmentary memories, and intermittent questions to Willie whose conversation is limited to a few curt replies and two or three scraps which he reads aloud from the newspaper.

At the opening of the play Willie is asleep, unseen behind the mound, but soon he sits up and reads the newspaper. His announcement that a Dr Carolus Hunter has died in a tub triggers off a few girlhood memories of Winnie's. After he has finished the paper he gloats over an obscene postcard which is seized by Winnie who examines it closely while registering conventional disgust. During Act 1 Willie gives brief answers to her questions, and finally returns to his newspaper and reads out again the advertisements for a smart youth and a bright boy, thus finishing the day as he began it.

Winnie's relationship with Willie is not one of love, in spite of her many sentimental phrases, for in fact she mocks him cruelly and alludes rather bitterly to his unresponsiveness: 'Oh I know you were never one to talk, I worship you Winnie be mine, and then nothing from that day forth only titbits from *Reynold's News*.' But although Willie is so uncommunicative, and moreover is placed so inconveniently that she has to bend back sideways to see him at all, yet he is absolutely necessary to her, for he is the indispensable Witness to her own personal existence; without him she would lose her identity. 'Just to know that in theory you can hear me though in fact you don't is all I need.' He is the Other who is needed to give reality to the self. As long as he is there as a potential listener she can babble on, quote scraps of misremembered poetry, or tell herself a story.

There is one puzzling event in this act: the parasol inexplicably bursts into flames, presumably a case of spontaneous combustion caused by the intense heat. Winnie's reaction to this phenomenon is odd; she thinks that this 'happening' must have occurred before, though she cannot recall it, and then she remarks: 'Something has seemed to occur, and nothing has occurred, nothing at all . . . the sunshade will be there again tomorrow, beside me on this mound, to help me through the day.' And as further illustration of this kind of unreal event she breaks her mirror and throws it away, declaring that it will be in her bag again tomorrow. And indeed at the beginning of Act 2 the parasol is there on the mound intact again, so that (as once before in *Watt*) 'A thing that was nothing has happened, with the utmost formal distinctness.'

Another obscure passage in Act 1 relates to an incident when a man called Mr Shower or Cooker appeared with his wife and stood gaping at Winnie, commenting on her queer situation, asking what it all meant and why Willie did not dig her out. They then departed, and these were the last human beings Winnie ever saw. The fact that they carried bags and appeared as if from no-where, and then continued their journey leaving everything just as they found it, reminds one of the interlude of Pozzo and Lucky. Here perhaps the incident is meant as a phantasy symbolizing the indifference of the outside world to another person's misfortune. Perhaps also Mr Shower and his wife are another aspect of Willie and Winnie themselves, their aspect in the commonsense outer world as opposed to that in the phantasy world presented in the play.

When the curtain rises on Act 2 we should realize that some years have passed, for the mound, symbolical of the accumulating days of her life, now buries Winnie up to her neck; she cannot move her head, nor, of course, fiddle with her possessions, but only indicate with her eyes that she thinks of the bag on her left or the parasol or revolver which lie on her right. As the bell rings she wakes up and exclaims 'Hail holy light', but she does not pray as before. Soon she calls to Willie, who does not answer, and she reveals that she has not heard or seen him for a long time. She inverts the familiar 'Witness' theme: 'I used to think that I would learn to talk alone . . . but no. . . . Ergo you are there,' which is also a nice distortion of Descartes' formula into 'I talk therefore you exist.' She will even accept that he may be dead, like all the others, but still he is there because she is talking to him. And this leads to the riddle of Time, the mental difficulty of understanding the meaning of *then* and *now*, which also connects with the puzzle of a continuous personal identity. 'To have been always what I am—and so changed from what I was.'

After these very real metaphysical problems she tries to conjure up some awareness of her own physical features—her arms and breasts seem unreal because submerged, but she can just see the tip of her nose, her pouting lips and her tongue. What comforts her most, however, is seeing the bag on her left and the revolver on her right, the one a reminder of past happy days, the other a potential refuge (though she can never grasp it) for the time when words will fail her. She is also consoled by the fact that her mind has not yet failed her: 'I have not lost my reason—(Pause) not yet—(Pause) not all—(Pause) some remains.' Then, after telling herself a story about a child called Mildred (her daughter, herself, or wholly imaginary?), she reverts to the visit of Mr Shower and his wife, tries to continue the story of Mildred, and looks forward to the bell to sound for sleep.

The end of the play approaches when Willie—now a decrepit old man—appears, miraculously clad in morning dress, top hat, and white gloves, crawling on all fours round the mound which he tries unsuccessfully to climb. Winnie mocks him cruelly. 'Reminds me of the day you came whining for my hand . . . what a get-up, you do look a sight!' As he vainly tries to approach she offers to cheer him on, but something in his look suddenly frightens her and she wonders if he is mad. However when he just manages feebly to utter the syllable *Win* she is transported with joy.

'Win! (Pause) oh this *is* a happy day, this will have been another happy day! (Pause) After all. (Pause) So far.' She sings the Waltz Song from *The Merry Widow*—the tune of which we heard on her musical box during Act 1—while Willie on all fours gazes at her. Then they go on gazing, she smiling at him at first but suddenly switching the smile off, and after a long pause the curtain drops.

We do not see the expression on Willie's face which so scared Winnie. Was it just that of a dying old man, or was it murderous or suicidal—for the revolver was deliberately made conspicuous on the mound and his efforts to climb up may have been directed to it rather than to Winnie. So it remains one more ambiguity, like Moran's encounter with the shepherd, or Mr Rooney's possible guilt.

# Play

Unlike the previous dramas, this one is closely linked with *The Unnamable* and *How It Is*, for it is set in Limbo and its characters are the psi-components of three deceased people. This fact necessitates a very radical innovation in theatrical technique and the abandonment of some of the fundamental assumptions on which dramatists and actors normally work. All action, movement, gesture and facial expression are abolished; the three actors are imprisoned in funerary urns with only their heads visible and they are instructed that their faces are to remain impassive. The only remaining art by which an actor can interpret his lines, namely by the inflections of his voice, is also mainly eliminated, for he is told to utter his lines rapidly in a toneless voice almost throughout. When all three speak simultaneously their chorus is to be rather faint and 'largely unintelligible' in spite of the fact that it is highly significant and very carefully constructed; but this only becomes apparent when one reads the text.

One may ask what is achieved by this deliberate exclusion of all the actor's arts of expression and this sacrifice of immediate intelligibility? The answer, I think, is that it is necessary for the de-personalization of the characters, who in life had 'never been properly born' but had lived spuriously on unreal conventions and clichés. They had never achieved a unique personality, the true expression of an individual self, nor made any real contact with any other person. Almost all previous dramatists have worked so that their characters should appear as real individual personalities, clearly differentiated and interacting in various situations of conflict. Beckett had the opposite task of revealing the inner emptiness of these pseudo-personalities, so that the lines, which spoken normally would be charged with feeling, have to be rendered as if by a mechanical robot.

When the curtain rises a faint light reveals the urns with the three impassive faces, a man, his wife and his mistress, who gabble softly a short chorus which, since we do not distinguish the words, simply produces an impression of confusion. Actually this chorus is a polyphonic composition on themes derived from *The Unnamable*, the longing for darkness and silence and for the peace of total oblivion, and the confusion of a mind which wonders if perhaps it is not quite sane. When the man hopefully says (of this final peace) 'it will come,' his wife echoes him with 'but it will come,

the time will come,' though she is referring to the inevitable return of the light which plagues her; and the man's 'not merely all
over' is answered by her 'all over, wiped out,' which forms a
closing concord with his final words 'but as if never been.' The
musical structure of this chorus is further revealed by the dis-
cordant clashes—the man's hiccup, the giggle of his mistress, and
the wife's angry cry to the light to keep off her—which intervene
between the opening statement of the three themes and their
final concordant resolution.

This gabbled opening chorus takes only a few seconds, and
then the light is turned on full and the three start talking simultaneously but are stopped almost immediately by a blackout lasting five seconds.

Now the spotlight plays on each face in turn, switching rapidly
from one to another, and as each is illuminated he or she wakes to
consciousness and speaks. The light is, in fact, the light of consciousness, and human consciousness involves thought which in
its turn involves words and ultimately their utterance. 'You must
say words, as long as there are any,' said the Unnamable. The spotlight acts as an 'unique inquisitor' who forces each temporarily
conscious mind to speak. As it switches from one face to another
they narrate by turns in broken fragments their sordid little story
of adultery, which seems to have been the only memorable episode
in their empty lives. Each relates a few scraps from his or her
point of view and largely in clichés. The effect is rather as if in a
trio the vocalists were not to sing simultaneously but instead we
heard one bar of the bass part, followed by one from the soprano,
and then one from the contralto, and they continued thus in three
staggered lines of one bar song followed by two bars rest.

After enough of the story has been told the light dims for a
moment, and when the full spot is resumed the voices speak
mainly about their present condition and the demands which the
light seems silently to make of them, though they cannot guess
just what it wants them to say.

The man reflects that he had at first supposed that now all the
pain and worry of life was over peace would ensue and the past
would be obliterated. In spite of the intermittent spotlight he
clings to the idea that this is only a transitional stage which will
soon be replaced by total oblivion. He realizes the basic unreality
of his former life, that it was just play, and then asks 'when will all
this have been—just play?'

His thoughts then turn to the two women, who, he imagines,

may now be friends gossiping and comforting each other over a cup of tea. The banality is re-enforced by his reference to their fondness for green tea and his own preference for Lipton's. Then he reverts to the spotlight which seems to be demanding from him some statement which he is unable to formulate. Finally he decides that the spotlight is 'Mere eye, no mind' and despairingly asks 'Am I as much as . . . being seen?'

This last sentence, expressing the fundamental need of being witnessed, is paralleled in the reflections of the mistress. At first she is a little disappointed by death for she finds her condition more confusing and less restful than she had anticipated. She hopes that the light will get tired of wakening her back to consciousness; but she also admits the possibility that it may lose patience, get angry with her, and drive her out of her wits. Still, she decides that after all it may be quite meaningless and that perhaps no one is looking at or listening to her.

'Is anyone bothering about me at all?' she asks. Finally she questions whether she may be somewhat unhinged, but concludes with 'I doubt it' and an hysterical laugh.

The wife's reaction to the light is more agitated; she implores mercy and shouts at the spot to keep off her. She has a conscience which makes her feel that there must be something she has to say, or perhaps some action she must perform, such as biting off her tongue, to placate the spot before it will leave her alone to the darkness and silence which she longs for. She was prepared for penitence and 'at a pinch, atonement,' but concludes that these are not the point, that in fact no one is demanding anything of her, and that she must be content with the brief intervals of oblivion which the intermittent spotlight allows her.

The end of the play is reached with the man's key line: 'Am I as much as . . . being seen?' but at once the gabbled chorus starts up again and the whole play is repeated *da capo*. After the repeat there is a brief coda consisting of the initial trio:

{ 'I said to him, Give her up . . .'
{ 'One morning as I was sitting . . .'
{ 'We were not long together . . .'

And the man repeats his line as a solo,

'We were not long together . . .' to be followed by the final blackout and curtain.

This repetition of the whole play, as if it were a minuet by Mozart, achieves two ends. In the first place it enables the audience to hear and grasp the significance of many phrases which they inevitably missed because of the rapid delivery of the actors and the fragmentary presentation of the three independent monologues. What may be called the 'staggered polyphony' of the composition is so unfamiliar that unless one has first read the play one would not get half the points on a single hearing of it.

Secondly, the repeat emphasizes the interminable repetitive nature of this post-mortem existence. One realizes that the final darkness and silence of annihilation, making all as if it had never been, will never come to these three lost souls, any more than it did to the Unnamable or to Pim.

# Twelve

# 'The Unwitnessed Witness'

IN HIS LATER WORK Beckett has produced a number of very brief pieces for radio, television and stage, in which he presents a theme with the bare minimum of words and actions. His elliptical style evokes ideas and feelings rather than explicitly stating them, and it leaves much to the imagination of the viewer or reader. An extreme example of this is the 'dramaticule' *Come and Go* (published 1967) on which any commentary would be longer than the text. In this playlet three spinsters attempt to re-live the only portion of their past lives which they feel was vital and valid, that short portion of their adolescence when, schoolgirls, they used to sit holding hands on a log in the playground dreaming of the love which, alas, they were destined never to find in reality.

## Words and Music

In the volume containing *Play* there are two short pieces for radio, *Words and Music* and *Cascando*, in which a central self seems to direct two semi-independent functions of himself, thought and emotion, represented by Words or Voice and Music.

The first of these begins with Music tuning up and Words protesting against this, for emotion and thought are hostile to one another. As the tuning-up dies down Words embarks on a pseudo-learned discourse on Sloth as a powerful passion; this is strongly reminiscent of Lucky's famous speech.

Croak, an old man, is now heard shuffling in, and he calls to both the parties, who answer very humbly, and orders them to be friends. Then he commands Words to speak about Love, and Words obliges with some more of his automatic verbiage until he breaks off because he is sickened by the accompanying sentimental music.

They are called to order by Croak, and Words is made to change his theme to Age. This time, with the help of evocative suggestions from Music, he succeeds in composing a poem. The first stanza pictures an old man shivering by the embers, waiting for the hag who tends him to put the warming-pan in the bed and give him his toddy. It then evokes the memory of a past, idealized love, the face seen in the ashes, reminding us of Krapp's girl in the punt. The second stanza, alas, somewhat debases the ideal, for the music becomes more erotic and the poem more sensual. Words himself is shocked by what he has been seduced to say; Croak, presumably unable to endure the nostalgia, shuffles away; only Music is delighted with its performance.

Words, having lost the battle, capitulates and implores Music to repeat the sensuous themes while, unable to speak any more, he can only give a deep sigh.

## Cascando

In the second radio piece there is a very similar cast. The central self-conscious self is called the Opener; the intellectual function is a Voice; and the emotional function is again Music.

In this piece Music is simply an accompaniment to the Voice, not a rival. The Voice is under the compulsion of telling a story which, as in the *Trilogy*, shall both explain, and put an end to, existence. The style is rather that of *How It Is*, while the content is like a skeleton version of the stories in the *Trilogy*. One Woburn wanders alone over the country, with his old coat and stick, often falling flat in the mud or on the shore, and finally lying face down in the bilge in a boat which is drifting out towards an island, just as was pictured in the tramp's final vision at the close of the *Three Stories*.

The Opener is the prime-mover of Voice and Music; he sets them going and stops them at will, and this action constitutes his whole existence. He merely switches on and off the emotional and intellectual processes without having any notion of what they will produce. In this he differs from the more anthropomorphic Croak who dictated to Words the themes to be elaborated.

The piece comes to an end, but not to a conclusion of the Woburn Saga, with the Music playing, the Voice saying 'We're there . . . nearly . . . just a few more . . . Come on. . . .' and the Opener (like Pim) exclaiming fervently 'Good.'

In the volume containing *Eh Joe* there are two other short pieces. The first is a mime for two actors, entitled *Act Without Words II*. It symbolizes the emptiness of a life which consists of an alternation between the two split portions of a man—the introspective brooding inner self and the busy time-ridden outer self, whose identity is made clear by the fact that they each wear the same garments in turn. First one, then the other, is prodded into life, performs trivial actions, moves various objects but (as with the porter moving the milk-cans in *Watt*) achieves precisely nothing thereby.

# Film

The other work, *Film*, requires some preliminary explanation before a viewer would be likely to grasp its purpose. It attempts to embody visually, without any verbal text, the philosophical doctrine *Esse est percipi*, to be is to be perceived, with the rider that if all outside perception, by animals, people or God, is abolished one still continues to exist because there is no escape from one's own perception of oneself.

In order to present this idea the protagonist is split into O (the object), the person who is perceived, and E (for Eye, played by the camera) the perceiving self. In the film the man, O, is continually trying to avoid being perceived, in the street, on the stairs, and in his room; but it is in vain that he puts the cat and dog out, covers up the parrot and the goldfish, takes down the picture of God the Father, and smashes the mirror; he is still perceived by E.

He settles down in his rocking-chair to get rid of the remaining possible witnesses, seven photographs of himself at earlier stages. It is interesting to learn from Beckett's notes that the first two repeat an 'image' from *How It Is*. No. 1 shows a six months' old infant in his mother's arms, 'Her severe eyes devouring him. Her big old-fashioned beflowered hat.' And No. 2 is the four-year-old boy kneeling on a cushion saying his prayers with 'Mother on a chair beside him . . . severe eyes, similar hat to No. 1.'

The other photographs show the schoolboy, the graduate, the lover, the soldier, and lastly the man of thirty with a grim expression wearing a patch over his left eye.

After inspecting these records of his development he tears them all up and settles down to sleep hoping (like Murphy) to achieve the bliss of unperceived non-being. But the self-perceiver,

E, is still there and his gaze wakens O, whom we now see full face for the first time and realize he has a patch over his left eye. O now gazes upwards at E (who is looking down at him from the wall) and we see E's expression is one of unemotional intense concentration, whereas O's face has an expression of agony. Finally O sits bowed forward holding his head in his hands.

*Film* was produced in 1964 and won the Prix Filmcritica at Venice in 1965 and also the Special Jury Prize at the International Film Festival at Tours in 1966. Buster Keaton played the part of O.

Now that we have surveyed all the published novels and plays we may attempt a brief summing-up. As has been shown in some detail, the fundamental feature of Beckett's characters is that they are schizophrenic, in the accepted clinical sense of the word, or at the least are definitely schizoidal types. And the important fact about his presentation of these characters is that, unlike the traditional novelist, he does not merely report their behaviour from the point of view of an outside observer, but imaginatively describes their subjective experience of psychosis as it appears to their disturbed minds.

The facts of schizophrenic splitting at once raise profound questions about the nature and reality of the personal self; is there a unitary 'soul' or 'person', separable from the body, or only a complex entity made up of various bodily and mental component functions? Or indeed does the word *self* stand for an unreal concept which has no actual content? These questions have been asked and answered variously by philosophers, psychologists, mystics and others; they are not answered by Beckett but they are present in all his works. His characters either feel, like Mrs Rooney, that their personal identity is just a 'big pale blur', or in more severe cases that their life consists of a vain but inescapable search for a real self.

Connected with all this is the question of our relationship to, and our perception of, the external world, including of course other persons. Like the mystics, the psychotics reject the commonly accepted 'sane' view that reality consists of what we perceive with our five senses together with what we reasonably infer from these data. The mystic does not deny the reality which ordinary men accept but to him, in an ecstatic state, it may appear transfigured and irradiated with bright light. His self seems to expand to include a much wider, deeper self, and he is filled with a sense of security and peace; and on his return to 'normality' he retains a conviction as to the ultimate rightness of the universe. It is quite otherwise with the schizophrenic whose self is disrupted; for him the external world becomes, to a larger or smaller extent, unreal. His ego (which is the part of his psyche that relates him to the outer world) diminishes and may seem to vanish; internal chaos and confusion ensue and his visions may be of darkness and demons—the universe appears hostile and intrinsically evil.

Beckett's characters are full of this confusion and are acutely aware of the hostility of the outer world from which they seek to protect themselves by bodily flight from people and by mental flight into phantasy. But they are always searching for that immanent central self which they posit as the basis of those 'homeless mes and untenanted hims' that are the manifestations of their fragmented personalities. This central self goes under many names: In the twelfth *Text for Nothing* the tramp, realizing the inadequacy of a human witness (since his reality too is equally in question), postulates the need for a god, an 'unwitnessed witness of witnesses', who would be this central self, unmanifest but aware of the manifesting person. Murphy called it a 'matrix of surds'; Watt knew it as Mr Knott; Malone spoke of it as 'the other', and in *The Unnamable* M. calls it 'the silence'. In the first play it is the unseen, unknown Mr Godot for whom the tramps wait interminably—differing here from the heroes of the novels in that they do not search for this central self within themselves because they mistakenly conceive it as an outside power, at first as an important official who could help them but finally as a Jehovah who will probably punish them. Later, in *Play*, this central self is presented as an impersonal light, and in *Cascando* it is the Opener which switches off and on arbitrarily to animate the human puppet.

All Beckett's main themes converge round this concept of a central self being the only ultimate reality: life as mere 'play', a filling-up of time with futile actions performed by an unreal pseudo-self; birth as the original sin; the necessity for a witness to one's existence; the search for the real 'me', and the conviction that when found it will prove to be a void, a nothing which is the source of everything.

Throughout the works we find these themes and also the schizophrenic dichotomy of simultaneous assertion and denial of existence; the self is torn between the 'yes' of the will-to-live and the 'no' of the will-to-cease. In *Text VIII* the yearning of all the

K

Beckett heroes is epitomized in one profoundly tragic line: 'Ah if no were content to cut yes's throat and never cut it's own.' Only a poet acutely and intuitively aware of the co-existence of Eros and Thanatos in the human psyche could have written that line.

# Bibliography

## Novels and Stories

| | | Published in English |
|---|---|---|
| More Pricks than Kicks *out of print* | 1934 | *Chatto and Windus* |
| More Pricks than Kicks *limited edition* | 1966 | *Calder and Boyars* |
| (*One story*, Dante and the Lobster, *is reprinted in* A Beckett Reader) | | *Calder and Boyars* |
| Murphy | 1938 | *Calder and Boyars* |
| Watt | 1953 | *Calder and Boyars* |
| Molloy; Malone Dies; The Unnamable 1 *vol.* | 1959 | *Calder and Boyars* |
| Molloy *and* Malone Dies *also obtainable separately* | | *Calder and Boyars* |
| How It Is | 1964 | *Calder and Boyars* |
| Imagination Dead Imagine | 1966 | *Calder and Boyars* |
| No's Knife (*containing* Three Stories; Texts for Nothing; Imagination Dead Imagine; Ping; Enough; From an Abandoned Work) | 1967 | *Calder and Boyars* |

## Plays

| | | |
|---|---|---|
| Waiting for Godot | 1953 | *Faber and Faber* |
| Endgame; Act Without Words I | 1958 | *Faber and Faber* |
| All That Fall | 1957 | *Faber and Faber* |
| Krapp's Last Tape; Embers | 1958 | *Faber and Faber* |
| Happy Days | 1961 | *Faber and Faber* |
| Play; Words and Music; Cascando | 1964 | *Faber and Faber* |
| Eh Joe; Act Without Words II; Film | 1967 | *Faber and Faber* |
| Come and Go | 1967 | *Calder and Boyars* |

## Miscellaneous

| | | |
|---|---|---|
| Poems in English | 1961 | *Calder and Boyars* |
| Proust; *and* Three Dialogues | 1958 | *Calder and Boyars* |
| Dante-Bruno; Vico-Joyce (*In* Our Exagmination) | 1921 | *Faber and Faber* |
| A Beckett Reader (*selections*) | 1968 | *Calder and Boyars* |

## Criticism

| | | | |
|---|---|---|---|
| *Josephine Jacobsen and William R. Mueller* | The Testament of Beckett | 1966 | *Faber and Faber* |
| *Hugh Kenner* | Samuel Beckett | 1962 | *Calder and Boyars* |
| *R. N. Coe* | Beckett | 1964 | *Oliver and Boyd* |
| *John Fletcher* | The Novels of Samuel Beckett | 1964 | *Chatto and Windus* |
| *Martin Esslin (Editor)* | Samuel Beckett | 1965 | *Prentice-Hall Inc. N-J* |
| *(Various)* | Beckett at Sixty | 1967 | *Calder and Boyars* |

## Psychiatric

The following are useful paperbacks for the general reader:

| | | | |
|---|---|---|---|
| *R. D. Laing* | The Divided Self | 1965 | *Penguin Books* |
| *R. D. Laing* | The Politics of Experience | 1967 | *Penguin Books* |
| *D. Stafford Clarke* | Psychiatry Today | 1960 | *Penguin Books* |
| *Thigpen and Cleckley* | The Three Faces of Eve | 1960 | *Pan Books* |
| *Evelyn Lancaster* | Strangers in my Body | 1961 | *Pan Books* |
| *Leo Navratil* | Schizophrenie und Sprache | 1966 | *D.T.V. (No. 355)* |

# Indexes

# Index of Names
## (*Fictional in italics*)

# Index of Subjects
## *(Titles of works in italics)*